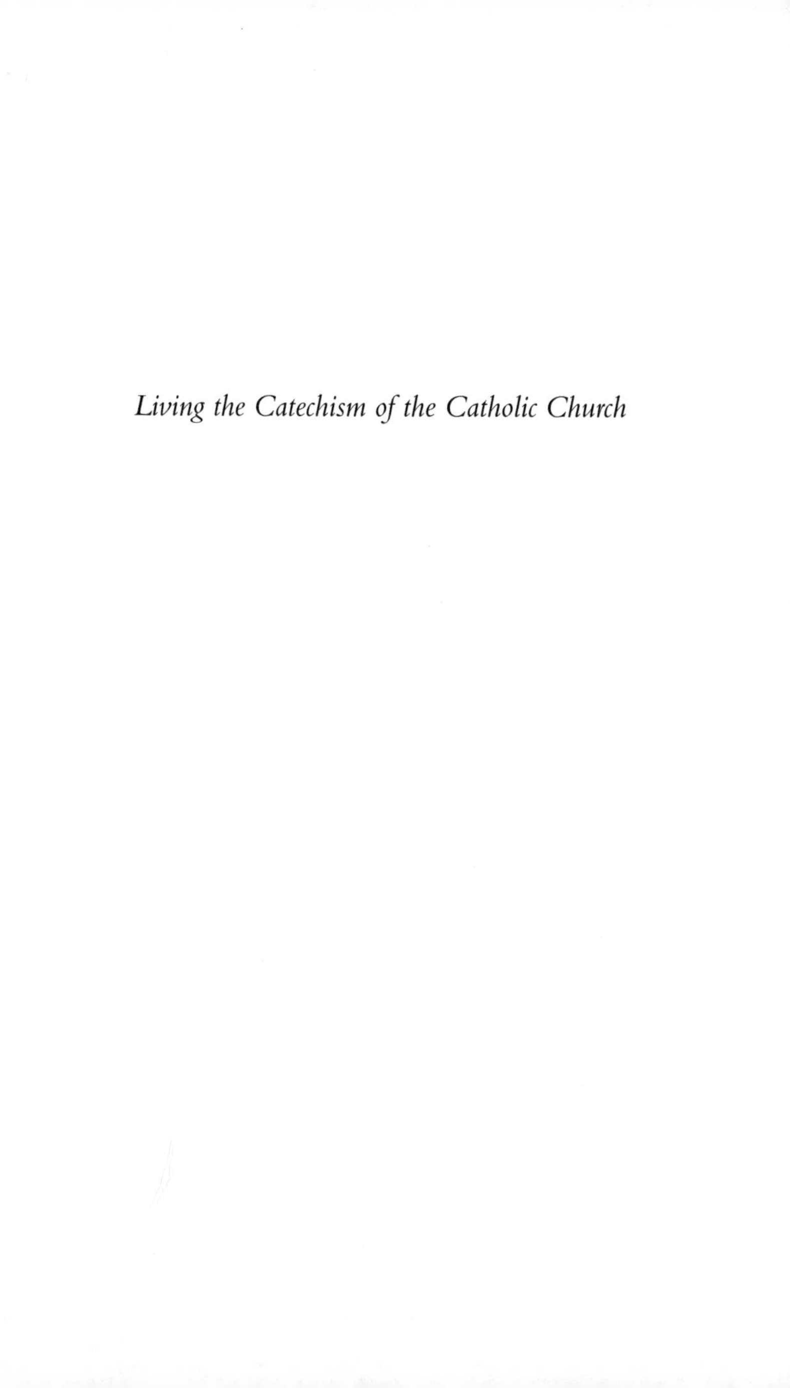

Living the Catechism of the Catholic Church

CHRISTOPH SCHÖNBORN, O.P.

Living the Catechism of the Catholic Church

A Brief Commentary on the Catechism for Every Week of the Year

Volume Two

THE SACRAMENTS

TRANSLATED BY JOHN SAWARD

IGNATIUS PRESS SAN FRANCISCO

Title of the German original:
Quellen unseres Glaubens
Liturgie und Sakramente im Katechismus der Katholischen Kirche

Cover design by Riz Boncan Marsella

ISBN 978-0-89870-727-4
Library of Congress catalogue number 95-75670
Printed in the United States of America ♾

For Joseph Cardinal Ratzinger
on his seventieth birthday
with gratitude and respect

Contents

Foreword

"Power came forth from him and healed them all." That is how Saint Luke the Evangelist describes the effect of Jesus on the many people who tried to touch him (Lk 6:19; 5:17; 8:45-47). What happened then to men in Galilee takes place today whenever men are touched by the sacraments of Christ. For, as the *Catechism* says, the sacraments are "powers that come forth from the Body of Christ, which is ever-living and life-giving" (*Catechism of the Catholic Church* [hereafter CCC] 1116).

It is with these healing and helping "powers", with the sevenfold wellspring of the sacraments, that the following fifty-two short chapters are concerned. As in the first volume [San Francisco: Ignatius Press, 1995], I have gathered together the weekly commentaries on the *Catechism* that I published in Vienna's archdiocesan newspaper, this time on the *Catechism*'s second part, "The Celebration of the Christian Mystery".

May this little book help to make the sacraments better known and lived as "the masterworks of God" in the new and everlasting covenant (CCC 1116).

+ Christoph Schönborn
Archbishop of Vienna

Feast of Saint Thérèse of Lisieux
October 1, 1996

I

What is liturgy?

"In Austria, at the present time", Adolf Holl recently remarked, "about 1.3 million Catholics go to church every Sunday. This means that Holy Mass is the most popular of all our public activities (cinema, soccer, theatre, and so on)." There used to be more people in church. There may be fewer in years to come. But one thing remains the same throughout the centuries: the faithful come together Sunday by Sunday, many also day by day, for the worship of God, for the celebration of the liturgy. The pagans of antiquity recognized this as the special mark of the Christians. In a letter written about A.D. 112, Pliny told the Emperor Trajan that, "on a certain day before daybreak", a large number of Christians came together "in order to sing antiphonally a hymn to Christ as to a god". From the beginning, the Church has been a community that prays and celebrates divine worship.

The Greek word for "liturgy" (*leiturgia*) primarily means "the performing of a service for the community" (cf. 2 Cor 9:12), but it can also mean "divine worship in public" (cf. Acts 13:2). As Christians understand it, the liturgy is first of all "the work of God" for men before it becomes our response of thanksgiving and supplication in divine worship. It is not in the first place we who "fashion" the liturgy. No, it is Christ who is the "liturgist", the "principal celebrant" of our divine worship. He has accomplished "the work of God" for us: our redemption and the glorification of God (CCC 1067). The great "liturgy" of Christ is the surrender of his life, the sacrifice he offered the Father on the Cross "once and for all" (CCC 1085), for us and for our reconciliation.

Every time the risen Lord celebrates the liturgy for us and with us, "the work of our redemption is accomplished" (CCC 1068). This is above all true of the Eucharist, in which Christ offers himself, together with his Body the Church, to God the Father.

Of course, the liturgy is not the Church's only activity (CCC 1072). The preaching of the Gospel and the service of neighbor by active love, personal prayer and sacrifice, the witness of Christian life, whether quiet or conspicuous: all these things are indispensable parts of the Church's life. However, "the liturgy is the summit toward which the activity of the Church is directed" (CCC 1074). The Rule of Saint Benedict says that nothing should take precedence over divine worship (CCC 347), though, of course, sometimes it is necessary, for the urgent needs of our neighbor, to forego attendance at divine worship.

Love of neighbor and the worship of God are not opposed. On the contrary, for the Church, the liturgy is "the font from which all her power flows" (CCC 1074). That is why it deserves the greatest care and reverence. Experience proves that wherever the Church's liturgy is celebrated in its simple beauty with dignity and love, the faithful come together. The liturgy is like a fountain in which the living wellspring that is Christ is contained and given to us to drink.

2

God the Father: source and origin of the whole liturgy

"Every good endowment and every perfect gift is from above, coming down from the Father of lights, with whom there is no variation or shadow due to change" (Jas 1:17).

The liturgy is first and foremost, as we have seen, "the work of God" for men. Our divine worship will always be a response to God's gifts. That is why there is always a two-way movement in everything that happens in the liturgy: a "descending" movement and an "ascending" movement, the first coming from the eternal Father, the source and origin of all life, and the second returning to him in petition, thanks, and praise. Hebrew, the original language of the Bible, has one and the same word for these two movements. The word *barak, bera'ha,* means both God's "blessing" and our "blessing", our praising of God in response. In Latin, in the words *benedicere* and *benedictio,* and in some modern languages, we discover this same double movement (CCC 1078).

Both meanings of "blessing" are expressed in the call of Abraham. God says to Abraham: "I will make of you a great nation, and I will bless you, and make your name great, so that you will be a blessing. I will bless those who bless you . . . and by you all the families of the earth shall bless themselves" (Gen 12:2–3). The man blessed by God becomes a blessing himself. Through his life and prayer he "gives back" to God his blessing by way of gratitude.

The Old Testament gives us many examples of such responsive blessings. They provide "prototypes" of the Christian liturgy. For example, when Moses tells his father-in-law how God has set his people free from slavery in Egypt and miraculously delivered them out of the hand of Pharaoh, Jethro rejoices and says: "Blessed be the LORD, who has delivered you out of the hands of the Egyptians and out of the hand of Pharaoh. Now I know that the LORD is greater than all gods." Then Jethro offered to God's glory a burnt offering and sacrifices, "and Aaron came with all the elders of Israel to eat bread with Moses' father-in-law before God" (Ex 18:8–12).

Here we find already foreshadowed all the essential elements of the Christian liturgy: the Liturgy of the Word calls to mind all the marvelous deeds of God; the Preface praises God for all his blessings; the sacrifice "embodies" thanks and supplication; the celebration ends with the meal, the sign of the presence of God's blessing. What is new about Christian liturgy is Christ himself. He is God's blessing, the Father's "perfect gift", and for him we "bless" God in the liturgy's song of praise. He is the gift at once of sacrifice and meal: "Blessed be the God and Father of our Lord Jesus Christ, who has blessed us in Christ with every spiritual blessing in the heavenly places" (Eph 1:3; CCC 1077).

"In the liturgy of the Church, God the Father is blessed and adored as the source of all the blessings of creation and salvation with which he has blessed us in his Son, in order to give us the Spirit of filial adoption" (CCC 1110).

3

The work of Christ in the liturgy

What do we celebrate in the liturgy? "We proclaim your death, O Lord, and we confess your resurrection until you come." Christ is the center of the liturgy. At Christmas we celebrate his birth, at Easter his Passion and Resurrection. We celebrate his Baptism and his Transfiguration, his forty days in the wilderness and his Ascension into Heaven. But "celebrating" here does not mean merely "recalling". It has the significance of a "now": in the Eucharist Christ's death and Resurrection are present; he himself is there. This is what is unique about Christian liturgy: it is Christ's work. In what sense?

"But when the time had fully come, God sent forth his Son" (Gal 4:4). *The* "work of God" is the sending of his Son. It reveals "the mystery which was kept secret for long ages" (Rom 16:25). It opens up the mystery of love that is God himself (1 Jn 4:16), the eternal communion of the Father, the Son, and the Holy Spirit. The final goal of all God's works is that we, and through us the whole of creation, be taken up into the communion of the triune God (CCC 260). To achieve this goal, God sent his Son "to unite all things in [Christ]" (Eph 1:10).

The "work" of Jesus, his life, death, and Resurrection, is the "great liturgy" through which the Father gives us his life, his grace (Rom 8:32). Christ is the real "liturgist" of this liturgy. It is he who has offered the Father the perfect act of divine worship. All his living and dying was "liturgy", the glorification of the Father (Jn 17:4). The Passion of our Lord took place "under Pontius Pilate". As a historical event it is a thing of the past. And yet, unlike other human happenings, it does not get drowned in the flood of history, for Jesus is risen and " 'always lives to make intercession' for us" (Heb 7:25; CCC 519).

Christ is risen. "All that he did and suffered for all men . . . participates in the divine eternity" (CCC 1085). His Cross and Resurrection are something perpetual, for in heaven "Christ permanently exercises his priesthood" (CCC 662). When we on earth celebrate the liturgy, we participate in this heavenly liturgy (CCC 1090). Then Christ is in our midst with all that he did and suffered for us.

The risen Lord is now with us in many different ways: through his Word, which, when it is read in the liturgy, he himself speaks to us; in the common prayer of the faithful, when he is "in the midst of them" (Mt 18:20); through his apostles and their successors, to whom he has entrusted "his power of sanctifying" (CCC 1087), especially in the celebration of the Holy Sacrifice of the Mass (for "the same now offers, through the ministry of priests, who formerly offered himself on the Cross"). Above all he is present under the Eucharistic species (CCC 1088). It is his liturgy; we celebrate it through him, with him, in him.

4

The power of the Holy Spirit in the liturgy

He is the Giver of Life! As Saint Augustine says, what the soul is for the members of the body, the Holy Spirit is for the Church (CCC 797). Everything in the Church that is truly alive, that lives with the life of Christ, has been raised to life by the Holy Spirit. His presence is, of course, hidden. His activity can be seen only by his fruits. The *Catechism* lists the four works by which we can know the Holy Spirit: he *prepares* men for the encounter with Christ; he *manifests* him and his words to men; he *makes Christ present*, and he *unites* men with Christ (CCC 737). This happens in a special way in the liturgy (CCC 1092).

True, it is we who celebrate the liturgy, and yet it is not a living thing because of all that we "do" or "organize" or "make up". The true power of the liturgy comes from the Holy Spirit, or rather, more exactly, from the cooperation, the "synergy" between the Holy Spirit and the Church (CCC 1091). This becomes clear when we think about his four workings.

If the liturgy is to be an encounter with Christ, we need *preparation*. Faith must be awakened, hearts opened. Only in this way are we enabled to receive the graces that our Lord wants to bestow through the liturgy (CCC 1098). No athlete or musician goes to work without preparation. God himself teaches us the importance of a period of preparation. Through the long history of the Old Covenant, he prepared the people of Israel and all mankind for receiving Christ (CCC 1093). That is why the Old Testament dimension must never be absent from the Church's liturgy. It is the school by which God guides us to the point of being ready for the coming of Christ (CCC 1094).

Our Lord promised that the Holy Spirit would "bring to [our] remembrance" everything that he said (Jn 14:26). "Remembrance" of the great things God has done is always an essential part of the liturgy (CCC 1103). In the Liturgy of the Word, we hear of the great events of the Old Covenant, and the words and deeds of Jesus are imprinted on our memory (CCC 1100). The Holy Spirit enables what we have heard to enter our hearts, to become vivid, alive, present (CCC 1101).

Yes, what is remembered becomes *really present.* This is most clear in the celebration of the Eucharist. Through the invocation of the Holy Spirit (CCC 1105) what the words of the liturgy call to mind ("On the day before he suffered . . .") happens here and now ("This is my Body . . . this is . . . my Blood"). What happened then is not simply repeated; it becomes present for us (CCC 1104).

When the Holy Spirit prepares us, when he brings to remembrance and makes present Christ's words and work, then we can reach the goal of everything that the Holy Spirit does: "the *fellowship* of the Holy Spirit" (CCC 1109; emphasis added). In every liturgical action, the Holy Spirit wants to unite the faithful with Christ, so that they may form his Body in brotherly communion (CCC 1108).

5

Christ in his sacraments

What is a sacrament? A sign perceptible by the senses, more exactly, a symbolic action, made up of words and gestures, that effects what it symbolizes (CCC 1084). For example, baptism consists essentially of pouring the blessed water three times, together with the words of the baptismal formula: "I baptize you in the name of the Father and of the Son and of the Holy Spirit." What is performed in the outward rite has an inward effect: baptism effects what the baptismal liturgy signifies—purification from sin and rebirth to new life in Christ.

The sacraments have their roots in the life of Christ. In his earthly life, Jesus often used signs and performed symbolic actions that illustrated his preaching (CCC 1151). In his healings and miracles, in particular, we find a kind of "prototype" of his sacraments (CCC 547). The *Catechism* highlights one example: the healing of the woman with the flow of blood (cf. the picture that introduces part 2 of the *Catechism*). The Gospels tell us that she touched the hem of Jesus' garment and was immediately healed. Our Lord for his part noticed that "power had gone forth from him" (Mk 5:30). The sacraments continue now what Jesus did then (CCC 1115). Through them and in them he "touches" us in order to heal us and give us his life. The sacraments are the "powers that come forth" from the

Body of Christ (CCC 1116). In each sacrament we encounter Christ, as men once met him on earth. He instituted the sacraments so that now, as the risen Lord, he might be with us in the lowly signs that are his sacraments.

Just as Christ then seemed insignificant to many people, as merely the carpenter's son (CCC 423), so now his sacraments often make an impression of something unprepossessing to those who do not look on them with the eyes of faith. For the divinity of Christ was hidden then, just as now the divine power in the sacraments remains invisible. We see water in Baptism, bread and wine on the altar, and yet in these visible signs the divine power of Christ is invisibly efficacious.

In fact, we touch the invisible reality of the grace bestowed in the sacraments only when we have faith in Christ himself, who is in a certain way the primordial Sacrament (CCC 774): in his human words and deeds his divinity is invisibly present. Our appreciation and feeling for the sacraments grow with our faith in Christ.

The Council says that the Church, too, is "like a sacrament" (CCC 775). She, too, is "essentially both human and divine, visible but endowed with invisible realities" (CCC 771). If we are to perceive in the often wretched outward form of the Church the divine life that pulses through her, we have to discover her as "Christ's instrument", as his "sacrament of salvation" (CCC 776), through which here and now he bestows healing and hallowing. In all the situations of life, the individual sacraments unfold the one sacrament that is the Church.

6

The sacraments of the Church

The Easter mystery is the foundation of our faith: "We proclaim your death, O Lord, and we confess your resurrection." Christ died for us; he is truly risen; he is present. What he once did in his earthly life, he continues to do, especially through the sacraments.

The Church teaches us that there are seven sacraments, and that these were all "instituted by Jesus Christ our Lord" (CCC 1114). In some of the sacraments both the fact that Christ instituted them and how he did so are obvious: for example, he gave the apostles the commission to baptize (CCC 1223), and, on the night before his Passion, at the Last Supper, he instituted the Eucharist (CCC 1337). We cannot for each and every sacrament locate an exact point of time when our Lord instituted it. However, all of the sacraments have "fixed points" in the life of Jesus, words and gestures of our Lord in which they are indicated and foreshadowed. A beautiful example of this is the anointing of the sick. Christ often uses sensible signs in order to heal. He touches the sick and lays his hands on them (CCC 1504). In her contact with the sick the Church very early on developed a special rite of prayers and anointing with oil (CCC 1510). Just as Christ then touched and healed the sick, so he does still through the sacrament of the anointing of the sick.

Only quite late (in the twelfth century) did the Church teach explicitly that there were exactly seven sacraments. The situation is similar to the fixing of the "canon" of Sacred Scripture (CCC 120). Here, too, during the first few centuries the Church considered, discerned, and in the end definitively laid down which writings from the early days of Christianity were to be regarded as composed under the inspiration of the Holy Spirit and therefore as the Word of God. Similarly, "the Church has discerned over the centuries that among liturgical celebrations there are seven that are, in the strict sense of the term, sacraments instituted by the Lord" (CCC 1117).

One of the characteristics of these seven sacraments is that they all have a certain relationship to the ordained ministry. This is especially clear in the case of the "Sacrament of sacraments", the Holy Eucharist. Celebrating the Eucharist "until he comes" is a mission that the apostles received from our Lord ("Do this in memory of me", CCC 1341). The "conferring of the sacraments" is entrusted to them and to their successors. When a priest absolves someone from his sins, he does so, not in his own name, but in the place of Christ, "in the person of Christ" (CCC 1461; 1548). Without the ordained ministry of bishops and priests, there would be no sacraments (the exception is emergency baptism, which can be performed by anyone; CCC 1256). The ordained priesthood is itself a sacrament, through which Christ builds up and leads his Church (CCC 1547). It "guarantees that it really is Christ who acts in the sacraments through the Holy Spirit for the Church" (CCC 1120).

7

Faith and sacrament

Had Christ not risen from the dead, there would be neither Church nor sacraments. He is at work in his sacraments. They are the signs and instruments of his presence. But they do not work without us. As the risen Lord said when he sent out his disciples into the world, "He who believes and is baptized will be saved" (Mk 16:16). The sacraments are not only conferred but also received. Their bestowal of grace and life does not depend on us, but whether we accept them and let them bear their fruit *does* depend on us.

The Church teaches that the sacraments are efficacious *ex opere operato*, "by the very fact of the action's being performed" (CCC 1128), that is, by the power of Christ, by the power of his Cross and Resurrection, and through the valid administration of the sacrament. When someone baptizes, he does not baptize by his own power; no, it is Christ himself who baptizes through him. Baptism does not have its effect according to our "mood", our feelings, indeed, not even through our faith, but by the power of the Paschal Mystery of Jesus. That, too, is the reason why the sacrament does not depend on the personal holiness of the minister. Even when a sinful priest—and which of us is without sin?—administers the sacrament of penance, it is in fact God himself who through him absolves me of my sins: "Since it is ultimately Christ who acts and effects salvation through the ordained minister, the unworthiness of the latter does not prevent Christ from acting" (CCC 1584).

And yet how I receive the sacrament is not irrelevant. Saint Paul reminds the Corinthians not to partake of the Bread and Cup of the Lord "unworthily", otherwise they will be guilty of profaning the Body and Blood of the Lord (1 Cor 11:27). But what is "worthy reception"?

First of all, it is reception in faith! The "Amen" by which we respond to "The Body of Christ" when we receive Holy Communion is a short act of faith, confirming my readiness to receive in faith what Christ wants to bestow on me in the sacrament.

This faith requires feeding and fostering. Instruction about the meaning of the sacraments is imperative. For each of the sacraments there is an appropriate form of preparation: catechesis for confirmation (CCC 1309) is as important for this purpose as the years of training leading to the sacrament of holy orders (CCC 1589). And how are married couples to know what it means for them to administer the sacrament to each other, for God to seal the bond of their marriage, and for Christ through the sacrament of marriage to be in their midst, if they have not been sufficiently instructed about the meaning of marriage (CCC 1632)? But preparation is necessary even for the sacraments that we receive frequently, such as penance and the Eucharist. Do we not often go to Communion with little thought or awareness (CCC 1385)? What we might call "post-preparation"—for example, thanksgiving after Communion—is also part of our fruitful reception of the sacraments, and in today's liturgy the time of silence that we need for this is often missing.

Ultimately our whole life contributes to the fruitfulness of our reception of the sacraments and to whether or not our hearts are open to what Christ wants to give us.

8

The sacraments: gates of eternal life

In each of the sacraments, past, present, and future are united at a point of intersection. All the sacraments recall a concrete historical event. Christian baptism recalls the Baptism of Jesus in the Jordan and, even farther back, the crossing of the Red Sea by the people of Israel: we are reminded of this "pre-history" of baptism in the readings of the Easter Vigil (CCC 281; 1221). This is particularly clear in the "memorial" in the celebration of the Eucharist: "Do this in memory of me" is our Lord's explicit command (CCC 1341). Something similar can be said of all the sacraments. They are rooted in the history of the people of God. They all have "points of contact" with the life of Jesus, from which they must never be separated. They are not just universal symbols of human life, but "signs and instruments" of Christ for us.

There is a passage in the Jewish Seder, the order of service for the Passover meal, which says that each of the participants should think of himself as someone who is even now setting out from Egypt.

This beautiful and profound thought is also applicable to the sacraments: they are not mere reminders of something in the remote past. When we remember what took place then once and for all (CCC 1085), it becomes present for today; we become participants in that past event. In the celebration of the Eucharist, when we do what Jesus commanded us to do until he comes again, what Jesus did and said at the Last Supper becomes present. We can even say that we become partakers of his Last Supper. It is as if time were done away with. Our Lord's sacrifice on the Cross is now present. We join him at table, we become his "contemporaries", we are in the Upper Room. Yes, the Eucharist is the presence of the Lord.

However, past and present are not the only dimensions of the sacraments; the sacraments also point to the future. To use an image of the Byzantine lay mystic Saint Nicolaus Cabasilas (*The Life in Christ* [Crestwood, N.Y.: St. Vladimir's Seminary Press, 1974]), the sacraments are the "gates of heaven" through which Christ comes to meet us. In his beautiful and profound book on the three sacraments of initiation—baptism, confirmation, and the Eucharist—this spiritual master of the fourteenth century describes how the sacraments in a certain way lead us into the future, how in them heaven already opens up to us. Saint Paul speaks of the Holy Spirit as the "firstfruits" of the glory to come. We can apply those words to the sacraments: they are a "foretaste" of heaven (CCC 1130).

A text of the early Church tells us how Christians waited for the Lord to return on the night of Easter, just as even today Jewish believers expect the Messiah to come on the night of Passover. Full of longing, the first Christians cried out "Maranatha", "Come, Lord Jesus!" When night ended and morning broke, and the Lord had not on that Easter night returned as he had promised, they began the celebration of the Eucharist. Does not Christ, the risen Lord, also come in the Eucharist? In a hidden way, of course, still in the pilgrim mantle of the Church. And yet he is with us always—today, in the humble form of the sacraments; on the Last Day, in his glory.

9

Who celebrates the liturgy?

Many people will answer this question: "The priest!" If they are thinking of the celebration of the liturgy of the Mass, then they are right, in the sense that without the ordained priest, there can be no celebration of the Eucharist. Others will say: "The whole Church, we all celebrate the liturgy." That, too, is correct, as long as we have the right understanding of "the whole Church". True, "it is the whole *community* . . . that celebrates" (CCC 1140). Liturgical actions are always "celebrations of the Church". The Second Vatican Council emphasized the communal character of all liturgical celebrations and spoke of the "active participation" of all the faithful in the liturgy. However, before we turn to the question of what this means for each individual and for the different roles to be played in the liturgy, we must point out a rather strange but very important fact.

The *Catechism*'s first answer to the question "Who celebrates?" is: "The *whole Christ*" (CCC 1136), Christ the Head with all his members. The "principal celebrant" is Christ himself. And the liturgy that he celebrates is his heavenly liturgy. We cannot take this idea too deeply into our hearts. The Council gave it vivid expression: "In the earthly liturgy we share in a foretaste of that heavenly liturgy which is celebrated in the Holy City of Jerusalem toward which we journey as pilgrims, where Christ is sitting at the right hand of God" (CCC 1090).

How aware are we that the earthly liturgy we celebrate in our parishes is a participation in the liturgy of heaven? Do we not always say at the end of the Preface in the Mass that we are joining our voices to the song of praise offered to God by the angels and all the saints in heaven? We sing the *Sanctus* with the whole Church in heaven. And when we remember in each Eucharistic Prayer the Mother of God and the saints, we do so "in communion with them" (Eucharistic Prayer 1). Our liturgical assembly participates in all the glory of the heavenly Church (CCC 957), even though we can make contact with this reality only in faith. What a breadth and depth this gives our worship! If Christ is in our midst, then present with him are all the members of his Body, and we are all united with one another: those already perfect with Christ and the pilgrims still on earth, those here present in our parish and all with whom we are united in faith. This is "the whole Christ" that celebrates the liturgy!

"Active participation", then, does not mean primarily as much outward activity as possible but, rather, inward involvement, by attentiveness and faith, in what is happening in the liturgy. Without this fervent sharing in the celebration from the heart, outward "active participation" cannot turn us into a real liturgical community.

By the same token, "the members do not all have the same function" (CCC 1142). As the Council says, in the liturgy each person should do "*all* and *only*" those things proper to him (CCC 1144). The ordained priest has his irreplaceable ministry, especially in the Eucharist and the sacrament of penance, of acting "in the person of Christ" (CCC 1142). The ministry of the deacon has been developing in recent years. And the living liturgy also draws life from the many other "particular ministries" that have developed since the Council (CCC 1143): readers, extraordinary ministers of Holy Communion, the people who lead Liturgies of the Word, and so on. The "unity of the Spirit" should unite everyone in the common worship of God.

10

Signs and symbols

In 1927 Romano Guardini published a little book, which has continually been reprinted, with the title *Sacred Signs*. Its purpose, still relevant today, was to facilitate "liturgical formation"—not abstract instruction, but vivid exposition of the simple gestures, signs, and symbols associated with the liturgy. Among other things he talks about kneeling and standing, steps and doors, holy water and incense, candles and bells, bread and wine, chalice and paten.

This handful of key words is enough to remind us that all these things, and many others, are part of the liturgy, even if we do not think about them in any special way. In Guardini's opinion, what matters most is not thinking about them but simply doing these sacred signs. A mother teaching her child to make the sign of the Cross, the simple gesture of taking holy water and genuflecting when we go into church—such "body language" speaks for itself.

Does it still do this? In his foreword to Bishop Kapellari's book *Heilige Zeichen* [Sacred signs] (Styria, 1987), Hans Urs von Balthasar said: "The simple things around us have largely lost their power to speak to us. And we who no longer hear what they have to say are like illiterates trying to read the book of creation." If we are to hear the language of the sacraments, we must first of all learn the language of things.

The *Catechism* reminds us that all sacramental signs have three dimensions. In the sacraments "creaturely" signs form the foundation (CCC 1146): water, say, or bread, "which earth has given and human hands have made", the fruit of the vine, oil. Maria Montessori, the great Catholic educationalist, got the children to help with preparing the bread and wine that they later presented at the altar. This kind of introduction is even more necessary today, when so many of us lack a living relationship with creation.

Sacramental signs are not, of course, just cosmic symbols. Their creaturely significance has been taken up into the history of God's people (CCC 1150). God gives his people "signs of the covenant" such as circumcision, sacrifices, Passover.

Christ uses both "natural" signs (for example, in his healings) and signs from the Old Covenant (for example, at the Last Supper), and both acquire a new meaning (CCC 1151): they become his signs, he himself speaks and is at work in them.

In the Church's sacraments these three dimensions are always present. If we want to deepen our understanding of the sacraments, it may be helpful to ask how far we are conscious of these dimensions and how clearly they are expressed in catechesis and liturgical celebration. The best "pedagogy" for sacramental signs is probably the fostering of "sacred signs". When the Paschal candle is carried into the deep darkness of the church, when light spreads from candle to candle, then this "creaturely" experience leads—not, of course, without faith—to "Christ our light".

11

Church music

In the last of the one hundred and fifty psalms it says: "Praise [the LORD] with trumpet sound; praise him with lute and harp! Praise him with timbrel and dance; praise him with strings and pipe! Praise him with sounding cymbals; praise him with loud clashing cymbals! Let everything that breathes praise the LORD!"

From earliest times singing and music have been part of the life of God's people. One cannot think of the Church without them. The words attributed to Saint Augustine are well known: "He who sings prays twice" (CCC 1156). In the Old Testament prayer-in-song expressed itself in many forms. They can all be found in the book of Psalms: praise and lament, thanksgiving and petition, pilgrim songs and meditations on the great works of God (CCC 2588).

The Psalms remain for all time the great school of prayer, and the important thing about them is that they are songs in which prayer finds its expression. In our German-speaking countries songs make up the very core of our Church music. They form a rich treasury of sung prayer. Many hymns have the "sound of home" about them. They are the familiar accompaniment of the various seasons of the Church's year, of Advent, of Christmastide (what an inexhaustible richness we have here, a sign of love for the mystery of Christmas, of the

Incarnation of God!), of Easter joy. Certain hymns to our Lady are like the sounds of the Church's heart.

In addition to the treasury of the Church's hymns, which are the "heritage" of the people of God, other forms of Church music have their proper place, their rights. There was a time when there was only congregational singing. Choral singing led to the faithful simply listening passively, in silence. Nowadays we have gotten beyond this one-sided view. The church choir has its rightful place as a precious element in the liturgical life of the parish. It is not a matter of passive "exposure" when the congregation listens to the singing of the church choir. In fact, listening can make our interior prayer with the Church even stronger, and when the choir performs a particularly beautiful and "devotional" piece, the whole congregation can experience what it means to say "Lift up your hearts!" That is why it is justified, indeed desirable, that solemn High Masses should occasionally be "performed", even with orchestral accompaniment, not for the sake of mere cultural pleasure, but to give glory to God and joy to man.

One disputed question is the use of modern "youth music" in the liturgy. I have experienced many so-called "folk Masses" at confirmations. These contain much that is moving but also much that is too cheap, lacking in quality. We should reflect on the fact that at the present time, among young people themselves, there is worldwide enthusiasm for listening to Gregorian Chant (for example, the CDs from Santo Domingo de Silos in Spain have enjoyed great success). Here is a buried treasure that we should restore. In these noisy times of ours this pure, profoundly spiritual music is like a "heavenly medicine". Here, from the very heart of liturgy, innermost prayer has become song (CCC 1157).

12

Liturgy and image

Do images belong to the liturgy? Many new churches are so bare, indeed so bleak, that one has the impression that images have been banned from church. In contrast, we have our Baroque churches with their superabundance of pictures and statues, which are a "feast for the eye" (CCC 1162).

For centuries there was struggle in the Church about whether iconic representations should have a place in the Church's liturgy. Is the Old Covenant prohibition of images (CCC 2132) still in force in the New? The Church answered this question quite early on. From the second and third centuries we find a wealth of paintings in the burial places of Christians, in the catacombs. There are depictions of the scenes from the Old Testament, from the life of Jesus, and from the Church. These early images are signs of salvation. They are meant to bear witness to the redemption Christ gives us. They are images of hope for eternal life (cf. the illustrations and the "logo" of the *Catechism*).

In the seventh and eighth centuries there was, of course, a violent controversy about whether the use of images in the Church meant a relapse into paganism, a kind of idolatry. At that time the Church gave a decisive answer, which remains valid to this day: through his Incarnation, Christ, the eternal Son of God, became true man and thus capable of being portrayed, represented in an image, with an unmistakable human face (CCC 476). The Old Testament's prohibition of images refers to the incomprehensible, invisible God. It also forbids the depiction of created beings (Ex 20:4) in order to avert the danger of idolatry (CCC 2129).

But in the New Testament God himself has given us his true Image: his Son, who became man (CCC 1159). Jesus says: "He who has seen me has seen the Father" (Jn 14:9). Christ is "the image of the invisible God" (Col 1:15). He is therefore "the human face of God".

But what reasons does the Church give for the move from the Incarnation of God to the permitting of iconic representations of Christ? The Fathers of the Church like to compare sacred images with Sacred Scripture: just as the Word of Christ is transmitted orally or in writing in the human words of his witnesses, so in a certain sense the face of Christ is handed on through the witness of the images of Christ. None of them is perfect, and yet there are many profound and moving images of Christ, in which something of his Person shines through (CCC 1160).

Today the question is asked: Does contemporary art have the courage, does it have the capacity, to represent Christ? Many people prefer symbols, abstract configurations, to an objective image. Nevertheless, I believe that we can never totally renounce the depiction of Christ, our Lady, and the saints. Images, too, belong to the liturgy, to the house of God, to personal piety. They help us to imprint Christ and his saints on our memories, so that we may always live in their presence.

13

"Today!"

On the day of Pentecost, in the Magnificat antiphon at Evening Prayer II, the Church prays as follows: "This is the day of Pentecost, alleluia. Today the Holy Spirit appeared to the disciples in the form of fire and gave to them his special gifts; he sent them into the whole world to proclaim that whoever believes and is baptized will be saved, alleluia!"

This "today" rings out on all the great feasts of the Church's year. Best known of all is the Christmas antiphon (Evening Prayer II): "Christ the Lord is born today; today, the Savior has appeared. Earth echoes songs of angel choirs, archangels' joyful praise. Today on earth his friends exult: Glory to God in the highest, alleluia!" (cf. Ps 118:24).

What is the real reason for this "today"? It is not confined to the great feasts but applies to every day. Day by day the Church begins the Liturgy of the Hours with Psalm 95: "O that today you would hearken to his voice! Harden not your hearts, as at Meribah, as on the day of Massah in the wilderness, when your fathers tested me" (vv. 7–9). The Epistle to the Hebrews explains this as follows: "[E]xhort one another every day, as long as it is called 'today,' that none of you may be hardened by the deceitfulness of sin. For we share in Christ, if only we hold our first confidence firm to the end" (Heb 3:13–14).

For believers, every day is this "today" of God. The reason for it is Christ himself, who said: "Lo, I am with you always, to the close of the age" (Mt 28:20). Since Christ rose from the dead, returned to the Father, and sent us the Holy Spirit, the time in which we live has been made new (CCC 1165). Time no longer runs away from us. It does not merely flow toward death but is filled with Christ's promise, "I am with you." True, we still live in time; we experience all of time's conflicts, from impatient waiting to the hectic shortage of time. We have to struggle with the organization of time, against the frivolous wasting of time, and for a responsible handling of the time that has been given us (cf. Eph 5:16), for a right understanding of the "signs of the times" (Lk 12:56), and for the right way to act at the right time, especially with regard to our neighbor (cf. Mt 25:40).

In these worries of ours about time, nothing helps us better than to live in the "today" of the Lord, who said, "Do not be anxious about tomorrow, for tomorrow will be anxious for itself. Let the day's own trouble be sufficient for the day" (Mt 6:34), and who taught us to pray, "Give us this day our daily bread" (Mt 6:11; CCC 2836). To live in this "today" is ultimately a matter of love. Saint Thérèse of Lisieux put it this way in a well-known poem: "My life is but a moment, an hour that passes by/ My life is just a day that flees and flies away/ You know this well, O my God! To love you on earth/ I have nothing but today! . . ."

14

The Church's year

We have entered "Ordinary Time". Eastertide is at an end. The "green" time has begun. It lasts right to the end of the Church's year, to the last Sunday in Ordinary Time, the Sunday of Christ the King. With the First Sunday of Advent, a new ecclesiastical year begins.

What is the significance of the liturgical course of the year? Is it an endlessly turning wheel, the same thing returning over and over again? Is each year the same, constantly repeated, the only difference being that as we grow older we have the impression that the years are passing more and more quickly? The great religions of Asia (Hinduism and Buddhism) see time as this kind of perpetual return of the same thing, as a great wheel that turns over long periods only to come back again and again to the same starting point. This view of time is bound up with the idea of rebirth or "reincarnation", which is widely held in these religions and is now very common in our own culture.

The Christian understanding of time is quite different. It finds its expression in the Church's year, and to share fervently in the celebration of that year imprints upon us a new "feel" for time. Liturgical time is defined by the one great event that makes all things new: the Pasch of Christ, his death and Resurrection. Since Easter, time has a new quality. It no longer runs toward death in the way our ordinary human life does. It is filled with the new life of Christ: "The mystery of the Resurrection, in which Christ crushed death, permeates with its powerful energy our old time, until all is subjected to him" (CCC 1169).

Anyone who celebrates the liturgy with the Church through the course of the year will discover that his understanding of time has been transformed. The year, the week, the day acquire a new "taste". They no longer "fade away". They become richer, denser, more filled with life. In this new time the feast of Easter is a source of light that brightens everything with its beams: it is the center and summit of the liturgical year (CCC 1168). From here the whole liturgical year unfolds: at the center the "Great Week" (as Eastern Christians call Holy Week), preceded by the seven weeks leading up to Easter (Lent, the time of Paschal penance), in which we prepare for our "regeneration" through the death and Resurrection of Christ, and finally the seven weeks of Eastertide, which are intended to insert us into the new life in Christ, culminating with Pentecost, when we are sent out by the Holy Spirit as his witnesses.

The second great group of feasts in the Church's year has at its center Christmas, the mystery of the Incarnation of God, his coming into our poor humanity, in order to bring us his light and his life.

In the course of the Church's year we celebrate all the great events of the earthly life of Jesus: his circumcision and presentation in the Temple, his forty days in the wilderness, his baptism and Transfiguration, and then, Sunday by Sunday, indeed, day by day, the words and deeds of Jesus as they are recorded in the Gospels. But in all this Easter is always the luminous source: the risen Lord in our midst.

15

Sunday

"On the day we call the day of the sun, all who dwell in the city or country gather in the same place." With these words, written in about 155, Saint Justin Martyr describes the divine worship of Christians (CCC 1345). From the beginning, the worshipping community of Christians on Sunday is one of the typical characteristics of the Church. And so it has remained to this day. Opinion polls and sociological research show time and again that there is a close connection between regular attendance at divine worship on Sunday and "ecclesiality".

The first day of the week, the day of Christ's Resurrection, is, in the words of the Council, the "original festal day of Christians". It is and always will be the first and most important day of the week for Christians. The "Sunday obligation", or "Sunday precept" (CCC 2180–83), results from an inner necessity of the life of faith. The Christian life of the parish stands and falls with Sunday, for the core of the Church's life is the coming together of her members for divine worship. The man who by negligence fails to observe Sunday will find it hard to preserve a living faith to the end.

"[Do not] neglect to meet together, as is the habit of some, but . . . encourage one another." This admonition in the Epistle to the Hebrews (10:25; CCC 2178) must refer directly to Sunday, though doubtless it also concerns the celebration of the "day of the Lord".

Sunday is the "day of the Lord". As the day of Christ's Resurrection, it is "a day of joy and leisure" (Constitution on the Liturgy). The celebration of the Eucharist is the center and summit of Sunday. Here "the whole community of the faithful encounters the risen Lord who invites them to his banquet" (CCC 1166).

These days the proper celebration of Sunday is endangered in a good many ways. The weekend, free from work, is, to be sure, a benefit and opportunity, but more and more it obscures what is special about Sunday. If only we would wish one another "Happy Sunday" instead of the now standard greeting, "Have a nice weekend"!

Because of the shortage of priests, the celebration of the Eucharist on Sundays is not possible in every parish. Liturgies of the Word, occasionally accompanied by the distribution of Holy Communion, should make it possible for the parish community to come together on a Sunday even without priests. Of course, given today's mobility, it is not difficult to travel to the places where Mass is being celebrated. In the early Church the faithful in town came together in "house groups", but they also assembled from all over, as the text quoted at the beginning shows, for the greater liturgical celebrations, especially on Sundays. Both of these things ought to be possible for us as well.

Sunday is the sun of the whole week. It should make our whole life "paschal". As Saint Gregory of Nyssa says, "for the whole week of his life, the Christian lives out the one and only Easter and lets this time become light." Origen, too, makes the same point: "There is not a single day when the Christian does not celebrate Easter."

16

The Liturgy of the Hours

Jesus instructed his disciples to pray without ceasing (cf. Lk 18:1; 21:36). This cannot mean that we should be perpetually engaged in explicit, vocal prayer, but it does mean, I think, that our hearts should be constantly with God, albeit by desire, by the yearning of the "restless heart" (CCC 30).

But "unceasing prayer" is made a reality by the Church. She, the Bride of Christ, is constantly at prayer, never concludes her praise, never silences her supplication, for the one Church prays in all her members, in those still on pilgrimage on earth and in those who have already been made perfect and one with God (CCC 954).

For Christians, there is, strictly speaking, no "private prayer". Each prayer, however personal it may be, is always an ecclesial prayer, since each of us, as a believer and as someone in the grace of Christ, is a living member of the Body of Christ. Whoever prays, prays in and with the Church, and the Church prays in each individual.

This combination of personal and ecclesial prayer is expressed above all in the so-called "Liturgy of the Hours". The practice of praying at certain hours of the day, and thus of sanctifying the "times of day", is to be found in many religions. Our Liturgy of the Hours is rooted in the Jewish tradition (CCC 1096). Already in the early Church we see the disciples gathered together at particular times for common prayer—at the third hour (Acts 2:13), the sixth (Acts 10:9), and the ninth (Acts 3:1); in other words, at nine in the morning, twelve noon, and three o'clock in the afternoon. We also see how they prayed and sang hymns to God "about midnight" (Acts 16:25). In addition, morning prayer and evening prayer are traditional among the Jewish people. It is good for us to reflect on the fact that the Church's times of prayer connect us with the root and stock of Israel (cf. Rom 11:18).

According to ancient Christian tradition, the Liturgy of the Hours is "so devised that the whole course of the day and night is made holy by the praise of God" (CCC 1174). The Liturgy of the Hours is the prayer of the whole people of God, even if not everyone can actively participate in it. The Council expressed the desire that at least the "principal hours", especially Evening Prayer, should be prayed in common in church on Sundays and the more solemn feasts (CCC 1175). In a good many places, on the eve of great feasts, a "vigil" is celebrated as a "gateway" to the feast.

But personal praying of the hours, with the help of a "Book of Hours" or breviary, is also the prayer of the Church. It is a happy fact that a growing number of lay people are praying the daily prayer of the Church, either on their own or with their families. The Liturgy of the Hours is a special obligation for priests, "because they are called to remain diligent in prayer and the service of the word" (Acts 6:4; CCC 1175). Prayer is the first apostolate, "for it is the Lord alone who can endow the work in which they are engaged with efficacy and success. . . . 'Without me you can do nothing'" (Constitution on the Liturgy, no. 86).

17

In the house of God

"A church, 'a house of prayer in which the Eucharist is celebrated and reserved, where the faithful assemble, and where is worshipped the presence of the Son of God our Savior, offered for us on the sacrificial altar for the help and consolation of the faithful—this house ought to be in good taste[1] and a worthy place for prayer and sacred ceremonial'" (CCC 1181).

But what is a beautiful house of God? The style of church building and the ordering of church interiors have undergone great changes: from the Romanesque church to the Gothic cathedral, from Baroque splendor to Gothic revival, from the beginnings of modern church architecture to today. But however different the styles, it is clear that at all times there were and are churches that are especially suitable for "prayer and sacred ceremonial", which in a most excellent way foster not only recollection but also the dignity of the liturgy.

The interior of a church is not just a container to be filled as we like. No, it is a living organism built up from its middle, its center. The heart of every church is the altar. It is a symbol, a sign, of Christ himself. Christ is the central point of every church, and it is around him that

[1] The official Latin, French, and German texts of the CCC translate as: ". . . this house ought to be beautiful . . ."

the congregation assembles. The center and summit of the liturgy is the celebration of his death and Resurrection. He himself is "Victim, Priest, and Altar" of his own sacrifice, which he offered to the Father for all mankind on the altar of the Cross. And so in the gifts we bring to the altar for the Eucharist we offer ourselves in order to be united with the sacrifice of Christ.

In earlier times altars were built above the graves of martyrs (for example, above the tomb of Saint Peter, in Rome). Today the relics of the saints are still kept in our altars. They are signs that Christian living and dying receive their strength from the one sacrifice of Christ.

The altar is also the "table of the Lord" for the Paschal meal, for which the risen Lord gathers Christians together in order to strengthen them with his Body and Blood. Christ's sacrifice and meal are inseparable, because his surrender of himself to the Father takes place for our sake, because he wants to give himself to us, so that we may live through him.

The ambo, which is the place of proclamation, is closely connected with the altar. Christ is also present in his Word. The Council speaks (in the singular!) of "the one table of God's Word and Christ's Body" (CCC 103). It thus emphasizes the inner unity of the Liturgy of the Word and the Liturgy of the Eucharist. In both parts of Holy Mass, Christ is the center.

An essential element in the furnishing of churches is the tabernacle. It should be situated "in a most worthy place with the greatest honor" (CCC 1183). Frère Roger Schutz, prior of Taizé, once wrote of the little Romanesque church in the village of Taizé: "This place is inhabited." He was referring to the tabernacle. This is what is unique about the house of God: the Lord himself dwells in our midst in the humble form of his Eucharist.

18

Liturgical unity and diversity

We have reached the end of our exposition of the liturgy in general. In the next part we shall enter the vast field of the individual sacraments. Before we do that, though, there remains one subject to consider, a subject with which the *Catechism* concludes the first section of part 2: the significance of the diversity of liturgical rites in the Church. Let us just mention the most important liturgical "families": the most widespread is the Roman rite, that is to say, the liturgy of the Roman Catholic Church; next comes the Byzantine rite, which is celebrated not only by the Orthodox Churches but also by the "Greek Catholic" Church (that is, the Churches of the Byzantine rite in full communion with Rome); finally, there are the smaller families of the Coptic, Syrian, Armenian, Maronite, and Chaldean rites (CCC 1203).

The diversity of these liturgical traditions was explicitly recognized and welcomed by the Council. They are entitled to "equal rights and equal honor." They should be preserved, promoted, and, in the spirit of sound tradition and according to the needs of the times, renewed.

In historical terms, this diversity developed from the "inculturation" of the Church among the different peoples, languages, and cultures of the world. It begins to appear from the Church's earliest times. Wherever the gospel goes, wherever churches are founded, an interrelationship is established between gospel and culture, between the missionary Church and the new believers. The different liturgical rites are the fruit of such "inculturation". They are "particular expressions", on which the culture has left its mark, of the one mystery of Christ (CCC 1202).

Anyone who occasionally attends a celebration of the Eucharist in the Byzantine rite discovers that it builds on the same basic structure of Holy Mass as the Latin rite, but in a different way, and that in both rites it is one and the same mystery that is celebrated. This diversity is an enrichment, as long as it is sustained within the unity of faith (CCC 1201).

All over the world today there is a discussion going on about the "inculturation" of the liturgy and of the Church in the various new cultures in which the universal Church is now living. In Africa and Asia "inculturation" has become one of the big issues. In our own culture, too, people ask whether the liturgy should keep in step with cultural changes.

The Gospel should be preached to all men, to all peoples, and thus in all cultures. In Psalm 2, which the Church applies to Christ, God says to the Messiah: "I will make the nations your heritage, and the ends of the earth your possession" (v. 8). Whenever a culture encounters the gospel, it is a kind of "homecoming", a return to the One who has been waiting for that culture in its very depths, that is, to Christ. Of course, this does not happen without a "conversion" of the culture, its purification from its "idols". The liturgy is the place where what is best in the cultures of the nations finds its way home to Christ.

19

Why seven sacraments?

Having commented on the section in the *Catechism* on the liturgy and sacraments in general, we now turn to the individual sacraments. The first question is: Why does the Church recognize seven sacraments, no more and no less? In chapter 6 we have already seen the sense in which we are to understand the Church's teaching that Christ instituted the sacraments of the New Covenant (CCC 1114, 1210). Today the question is why there are seven sacraments, why exactly *these* seven.

The sacraments give the Christian's life its beginning and growth, its healing and its mission. They touch all the stages and important moments of earthly life. That is why a certain analogy has often been drawn between the stages of earthly life and those of the spiritual life. Consider, for example, this text of Saint Thomas Aquinas (*Summa theologiae* 3a, 65, 1):

> The spiritual life has a certain conformity to bodily life. . . . Now in bodily life man is perfected in two ways: in one way, with regard to his own person; in another way, with respect to the whole community and society in which he lives, since man is by nature a social animal. . . . Of itself bodily life is perfected in three ways. First, by generation, by which man begins to exist and to live. Corresponding to this in the spiritual life is baptism, which is a spiritual

> regeneration. . . . Secondly, by growth, by which a man is brought to his complete size and strength. Corresponding to this in the spiritual life is confirmation, in which the Holy Spirit is given for strength. . . . Thirdly, through nourishment, by which life and strength is conserved in man. Corresponding to this in the spiritual life is the Eucharist. . . . And this would be sufficient for man, if, in body and in soul, he had impassible life. However, since man now and then falls sick both in his body and, through sin, in his soul, he needs to be healed of that sickness. This healing is twofold. First, there is the healing that is the restoration of health. Corresponding to this in the spiritual life is the Sacrament of Penance. . . . Secondly, there is the restoration of one's earlier strength and fitness through appropriate diet and exercise. Corresponding to this in the spiritual life is extreme unction [which since the Council we call the anointing of the sick]. . . . In his relations with the whole community, man is perfected in a twofold way. First, he is perfected by receiving power to govern the people and to exercise public acts. Corresponding to this in the spiritual life is the sacrament of order. Secondly, man is perfected with regard to natural propagation. This takes place through marriage, both in bodily and spiritual life, since it is not only a sacrament but also an office of nature.

Needless to say, this analogy does not exhaust all the aspects of the sacraments, but it does offer a true-to-life answer to the question in our title.

20

The sacraments of initiation

Three sacraments together form the gateway to the Christian life: baptism, confirmation, and (First) Holy Communion. Nowadays we very often do not realize that these three form a unity. Of course, anyone who witnesses the baptism of an adult will see this unity for himself. Usually, the adult candidate receives baptism, confirmation, and First Communion at the same time.

In the Acts of the Apostles we find cases of a very rapid initiation into the Christian life. Think, for example, of the conversion of the jailer in Troas: the very same night that he and his whole household became believers, he and they received baptism and the Lord's Supper (Acts 16:23–34). It was the same with the Ethiopian eunuch (Acts 8:26–40). But the early Church provides evidence for the fact that preparation for baptism was normally longer, up to three years. The catechumens (the candidates for baptism) received instruction, usually from the bishop himself, on the doctrine of Christian faith and morals. They learned the Creed, received the Lord's Prayer, and were examined on their manner of life and knowledge of the faith (the "scrutinies"). Exorcisms were performed to deliver them from the powers of darkness. Finally, usually at the Easter Vigil, they received baptism and anointing with holy oil. Now for the first time they were allowed to take part in the celebration of the Eucharist and to go up to the table of the Lord. Hitherto they had had to leave church after the Liturgy of the Word. Sharing in the celebration of the "mystery of faith" was reserved to the baptized.

Since the Second Vatican Council, the Church has restored this dynamic process of Christian initiation, taking the practice of the early Church as a model, and has established a proper "Rite for the Christian Initiation of Adults". It has worked out well, especially in countries where many adults are baptized.

In the fourth and fifth centuries, as the number of infant baptisms began to predominate, "initiation" fell more and more into oblivion. The Eastern Church preserves a kind of memory of it through its practice of conferring all three sacraments on infants. The Western Church has gone in a different direction. She has separated confirmation and First Communion from infant baptism, in order to connect the various steps of Christian initiation with the stages of young people's development. It is the task of pastors to explain the inner unity, as well as the salvific effects, of this sacramental way. Pope Paul VI puts it this way:

> The sharing in the divine nature given to men through the grace of Christ bears a certain likeness to the origin, development, and nourishing of natural life. The faithful are born anew by Baptism, strengthened by the sacrament of Confirmation, and receive in the Eucharist the food of eternal life. By means of these sacraments of Christian initiation, they thus receive in increasing measure the treasures of the divine life and advance toward the perfection of charity (CCC 1212).

21

Jesus' baptism—our baptism

Baptism is the gateway to the whole Christian life (CCC 1213). It is the basis of all the other sacraments. It is also "the foundation of communion among all Christians" (CCC 1271). But why do we need this rite to become a Christian? Is it not enough simply to believe in Christ, to entrust oneself to him and his Word? Are not the baptismal rites, performed with water and oil and candle, a kind of "magical relic" of a primitive age? What are the roots of baptism? And what is the meaning of its rites?

The roots of baptism (the Greek word *baptisma* originally means "submerging") go deep down into the earliest days of mankind. Water is one of the primordial elements of creation. Without water there is no life. Anyone who has experience of steppes and deserts knows how precious is the sound of a spring, what blessing there is in a shower of rain! Water not only brings life, it also cleanses, and since in man interior and exterior correspond to each other, bodily cleansing is also a symbol of the soul's renewal. But water in flood can also be deadly, sweeping life away and burying men beneath the waves (CCC 1217–20).

All three meanings flow together in baptism: deadly flood—baptism as a participation in the death and burial of Jesus (Rom 6:3–4; CCC 1227); cleansing—baptism as "the washing of regeneration" (CCC 1215); life—baptism as a resurrection with Christ to new life (CCC 1214).

Where does the Christian rite of baptism come from? With complete certainty we can say: from the very first day the disciples of our Lord baptized those who accepted the Word of proclamation, beginning with the three thousand converted on the day of Pentecost (Acts 2:41). Baptism was never questioned as the gateway to being a Christian (except by sectarian fringe-groups). The most obvious explanation for this is the assumption that Christians baptized from the beginning because they were commanded to do so by Jesus Christ (Mt 28:19–20; Mk 16:15–16), and because Jesus himself received baptism at the hands of John (CCC 1224).

The baptism of Jesus in the Jordan foreshadows not only the rite of baptism but also its significance. What moved Jesus to go down from Galilee to the Jordan in order to be baptized by John (Mt 3:13)? The Baptist hesitates to baptize the One who comes in the middle of a crowd of tax collectors, soldiers, and prostitutes, of Pharisees and Sadducees, as if he too were a penitent sinner (CCC 535). Jesus replies that for him it is a question of fulfilling "all righteousness" (Mt 3:15). Before the beginning of his public mission, his place is already fixed: in the midst of sinners. It is for them that he receives the baptism of repentance, and this baptism is the prefiguration of that other "baptism" with which he is constrained to be baptized: the giving up of his life "as a ransom for many" (Mk 10:45), "for the forgiveness of sins" (Mt 26:28). Our baptismal rite has its prefiguration in the baptism of Jesus in the Jordan. Its mysterious power and efficacy come from the Cross of Christ: we are baptized "into his death", so that he may implant in us his life (CCC 1225; 1227).

22

The baptismal rite as "mystagogy"

The rite of baptism speaks for itself. The individual words and gestures are so expressive that they do not really need to be explained at great length. In fact, commentaries are more a hindrance than a help—they get in the way of the direct impression that the ceremony makes. Of course, this all supposes that the various rites for administering baptism are celebrated clearly, reverently, and without haste.

It is a general principle: the sacramental rites signify what they effect. By outward signs they display the inward effect of the sacrament. That is why it is important to celebrate the words and gestures of the sacraments in such a way that they are "mystagogy", that is, an "initiation" into the mystery being enacted in the sacrament (CCC 1234).

It would be rewarding to study the baptismal rite of the early Church as described, for example, by Saint Ambrose, in his writings *On the Sacraments* and *On the Mysteries*, or by Saint Cyril of Jerusalem, in his *Mystagogical Catecheses*. Even though today's baptismal rite has become simpler, it has still retained the most important elements of the "mystagogy" of the early Church.

The celebration begins, wherever possible, at the church door, with the giving of the name and the request for baptism, for grace, for eternal life. The Word of God is meant to bring to mind the meaning of what happens in baptism and to elicit faith, which is inseparable from baptism (CCC 1236). In the early Church, the candidates made their renunciation of Satan facing west, the symbol of darkness, while their conversion to Christ was physically symbolized by their turning around toward the east, the rising light. And in our own time also this turning around takes place when the candidate says "I renounce" and makes his profession of faith. This is prepared for by the signing with the sign of the Cross, the prayer of exorcism, and the anointing with the oil of the catechumens. These should not be overlooked. The point is that in baptism the candidate is delivered from the power of darkness and plunged into the light of Christ.

Then follows the essential rite, baptism proper (CCC 1239). A great richness of symbolism surrounds this sacred moment. The consecration of the baptismal water (at the Easter Vigil or at each celebration) mentions the many connections to be found in Scripture between the baptismal rite now taking place and the events of salvation history. The baptismal font should be octagonal, to symbolize the eighth day of the new creation in Christ. In the past, and increasingly again today, baptism was usually conferred by a triple immersion, the sign of death and resurrection, but it was and is also conferred by pouring the water over the candidate's head, in the name of the Trinity. The anointing with chrism signifies and effects sealing with the Holy Spirit.

What has taken place in baptism is indicated by the rites that follow it, the clothing with the white garment and the giving of the candle (CCC 1242–43): the baptized person has "put on Christ" and has now become light. Of course, only faith in him who is at work in the visible rite will grasp this truth.

23

Why baptize infants?

Is it not better to allow each person to make his own free choice? We hear many parents say: "Children should decide for themselves, when they grow up." Other people think that infant baptism contradicts the explicit teaching of our Lord: "He who believes and is baptized will be saved" (Mk 16:16). Did he not mean by those words that personal faith must precede baptism? How can a baby receive "the sacrament of faith" (CCC 1236)? Is there not also a debate about whether the early Church recognized infant baptism? Is this not something that was introduced later by the "people's Church"?

There is evidence for the baptism of infants from the second century. The frequent mention of the baptism of whole "households" (for example, Acts 16:15, 33) probably means that infants were baptized at the same time. True, in the third and fourth centuries, we occasionally find reservations about infant baptism. The principal reason for this must have been the rigorous penitential practice of the time, which for grave sins imposed long, sometimes lifelong, excommunication and allowed only a single possibility of absolution. Many people, therefore, hesitated about taking on the yoke of baptism. Before being baptized, they preferred to wait till they had passed by the storms of youth and reached the safe haven of old age.

These days the objection to infant baptism comes not so much from fear of the heavy obligations that the baptized takes on as from the feeling that the infant does not yet need baptism. Behind both attitudes lies the same misunderstanding: the idea that baptism is a restriction of freedom. Both see baptism too externally.

Infant baptism is a "test case" for an understanding of the sacraments. If in the "sacrament of regeneration" we see first and foremost the action of Christ, his grace that is undeserved by us and always goes before us (CCC 1996), then infant baptism shows with special clarity that he loved us first (1 Jn 4:10): he died and rose again for us all, and this gift is bestowed upon us in baptism. Anyone who loves his child will not want to withhold baptism from him (CCC 1250).

But infant baptism makes another truth clear: that every human being is in need of salvation, even the newborn child. Because of original sin (CCC 403), no one is "healthy" in himself: health, the health that is salvation, is to be found only in Jesus (Acts 4:12). We are all in need of Jesus. It was for us all that he became man, our Redeemer. From childhood onward, he bestows true freedom.

"Let the children come to me, do not hinder them!" (Mk 10:14). How can we not bring children to him, who in the sacrament of baptism takes them "in his arms" and "blesses them" (Mk 10:16)? But infant baptism also brings with it the responsibility consciously and deliberately to bring the child to Christ through a religious upbringing. Where this is lacking, there is the danger that the grace of baptism will not be able to unfold. This makes it all the more urgent for us to bring the children to Christ (Mk 10:13).

24

The grace of baptism

The baptismal rite signifies what happens in baptism (CCC 1262). The senses, eyes and ears, perceive only the outward and visible signs. Only faith can perceive what is really happening in the baptized through these signs. The rite symbolizes two effects: death and regeneration. Both become a reality through baptism.

"Now faith is . . . the conviction of things not seen" (Heb 11:1). In baptism it is not primarily a question of an experience, but of a "profound effect", something of which we may very well have a "sense" but which is really grasped only by the depths of the soul, what is innermost in man.

Catholic teaching on the sacraments distinguishes a twofold effect of the sacraments. The first takes place immediately in the reception of the sacrament, while the other requires the cooperation of the receiver if it is to be unfolded. The first is given straightaway by Christ, while the other grows if we do in fact accept the gift of Christ. This important distinction makes it clear that the sacraments do not have any kind of "magical" effect. They are gifts of Christ, which, like the talents in the parable, we should try to increase.

Baptism, confirmation, and ordination imprint upon the recipient an "indelible spiritual mark (*character*)" (CCC 1272). This character signifies and effects one's belonging to Christ. The baptized man belongs to Christ; he is a Christian; he has been freed from the ancient fault and has become a "new creation".

Our faith tells us that no man is born righteous, that all have need of the Savior, of salvation. Jesus is the Savior of all men (CCC 389). That is why baptism is necessary for salvation (CCC 1257). "Unless one is born of water and the Spirit, he cannot enter the kingdom of God" (Jn 3:5). The gate to life is Christ himself. He has made baptism the entrance to his life. He himself can bestow this life even without baptism (for example, in the case of people who know nothing of the gospel). Nevertheless, he has mandated for us the way of baptism: "He who believes and is baptized will be saved" (Mk 16:16).

If baptism sets us free from our sins, why does the inclination to sin remain in the baptized? Manifestly, even after baptism, there is still evil within us. The Church teaches that the newly baptized is entirely free of all sin, but the "consequences of sin" remain: suffering, illness, death, but also weakness of character and above all "an inclination to sin", which is not itself something evil but is a kind of propensity for evil. That makes the life of the baptized a constant struggle not to squander the gift received in baptism (CCC 1264).

The baptized person is not on his own. He has become a member of the Body of Christ: "Baptism incorporates us *into the Church* (CCC 1267). If the grace of our baptism is to unfold, we need the whole communion of the Church: the help of the saints, guidance from our pastors, and fraternal love for one another.

25

Baptism and confirmation

"It must be explained to the faithful that the reception of the sacrament of Confirmation is necessary for the completion of baptismal grace" (CCC 1285). There is a close connection between baptism and confirmation, a connection to which we do not perhaps give enough attention. Let us first of all look at how this connection developed in history, and then we can discuss its deeper significance.

Anointing with the oil of chrism is also part of the rite of baptism (CCC 1241). It signifies sealing with the Holy Spirit. The baptized becomes an "anointed one", a Christian. Now he belongs to Christ, to the Messiah, the Anointed of God (CCC 1296). In Rome, from ancient times, it was the custom for this baptismal anointing to be completed or "confirmed" (strengthened) (CCC 1242) by the bishop when he anointed the newly baptized with holy oil on the forehead (CCC 1291). This rounded off baptism and enabled the baptized for the first time to participate in the Eucharist, to receive Holy Communion.

As the number of Christians increased in both town and country, this "confirmation" could not always be performed by the bishop immediately after baptism. As the bishop moved across the country, he confirmed all the people baptized since his last visit. Only then could they receive their First Communion. And that is how it was for many centuries, until in the last century the desire not to make children wait too long for their First Holy Communion grew stronger and stronger. Occasionally permission was given so that children did not have to wait for their First Communion till they had been confirmed by the bishop. When Pope Saint Pius X issued a general invitation to earlier and more frequent Communion, a change took place that to this very day is hard for our Orthodox fellow Christians to understand: those who have not been confirmed are allowed to receive Communion.

The Eastern Church has preserved the inner unity of the three "sacraments of initiation" in a very clear way by always administering baptism, confirmation (which is called *myron* in the East because of the sweet-smelling oil), and Communion together, whether the recipient is a child or an adult (CCC 1292). In our case, this unity is still clearly expressed when an adult is baptized (CCC 1291).

Why should there be a special sacrament of confirmation? The Protestant Reformers of the sixteenth century rejected confirmation as a sacrament, because they (for example, Calvin) thought that it was a disparagement of baptism to regard it as incomplete, as needing to be completed. When the connection between baptism and confirmation is forgotten, this criticism may have a certain force. But that is not the teaching of the Second Vatican Council. The Dogmatic Constitution on the Church states: "By the sacrament of Confirmation, [the baptized] are more perfectly bound to the Church and are enriched with a special strength of the Holy Spirit. Hence they are, as true witnesses of Christ, more strictly obliged to spread and defend the faith by word and deed" (*Lumen gentium*, quoted in CCC 1285).

26

Confirmation: age, sponsors, ministers

The question of the appropriate age for receiving confirmation is the subject of frequent discussion. All kinds of suggestions have been made. Many people would like to move confirmation back before First Communion, in order to restore the correct order of the sacraments of initiation. "In approximately the twelfth year"—that is the recommendation of the Würzburg Synod (1976). Others suggest early adulthood. "Always together with baptism"—so say the people who have the practice of the Eastern Church in mind. These wavering opinions seem to reflect a kind of uncertainty about the meaning of the sacrament of confirmation. This should stir us to reflection, even if we cannot come up with definitive answers.

The present Code of Canon Law tells us simply: "The faithful are obliged to receive this sacrament at the appropriate time" (CCC 1306). And it tells parents and pastors that they must ensure that the candidates for confirmation are well instructed and receive the sacrament "at the appropriate time" (CIC can. 890). For a long time the Latin tradition has said that "the age of discretion" (CCC 1307) is the appropriate age—which would suggest an early reception of the sacrament. On the other hand, the candidate for confirmation is supposed "to be able to renew [his] baptismal promises" (CIC can. 889 § 2)—does that not suggest a more mature age?

Saint Thomas gives us a clear warning not to approach the question of the right age for Confirmation in too rigid a way: "Age of body does not determine age of soul. Even in childhood man can attain spiritual maturity" (CCC 1308). He points to the many children who have witnessed to Christ by the shedding of their blood. "Christian maturity" is not restricted to the boundaries of age. It makes sense to adhere to a common "right age" (in Austria, the candidates have to be fourteen), but it is also important not to be too quick in setting restrictions of age on the working of the Holy Spirit.

Intensive preparation for confirmation in the parishes is a real gain, and it is now unthinkable that we could do without it. Through confirmation the baptized are "more perfectly bound to the Church" (CCC 1285), and so catechesis for confirmation should in a special way "awaken a sense of belonging to the Church" (CCC 1309). Of course, when this catechesis is done, there must be no neglect of the deepening of personal life with Christ under the guidance of the Holy Spirit.

The role of godparent is not essential to baptism and confirmation, but it is highly recommended (CCC 1255; 1311). It is also recommended that the person enlisted as a sponsor in confirmation should be one of the baptismal godparents: baptism and confirmation belong together. Today we are more and more aware that the whole community shares a responsibility for the faith journey of the candidates for confirmation.

The bishop, who is a successor of the apostles, is the "principal minister" of confirmation. Just as the apostles at Pentecost imparted the Spirit by the laying on of hands, so the bishop does through confirmation. Only when it is necessary should the priest be commissioned to confirm. Confirmation should strengthen one's bond with one's bishop.

27

The grace of confirmation

"What does confirmation add to the grace of baptism?", asked the late Cardinal Yves Congar, who had been a theologian at the Council. He went on to say: "Christian baptism is baptism in the Spirit; it gives us regeneration and takes us into the life of Christ, into his Body. That is what the liturgies say, as do the earliest Fathers. The Holy Spirit is already bestowed in baptism. Why, then, do we say that a further rite is needed for him to be given?" (*I Believe in the Holy Spirit* [New York: Seabury Press, 1983]).

The relationship between the grace of baptism and the grace of confirmation has occasionally been compared to the relationship between Easter and Pentecost. On Easter Day the risen Lord came into the midst of the disciples, gave his greeting of peace, and breathed upon them: "Receive the Holy Spirit" (Jn 20:22). On the day of Pentecost the disciples also received the gift of the Holy Spirit, as Jesus had promised after his Resurrection: "You shall receive power when the Holy Spirit has come upon you; and you shall be my witnesses" (Acts 1:8).

Both baptism and confirmation bestow the Holy Spirit and his gifts, and yet just as birth and growth cannot be reversed, so the sacrament of rebirth must precede the sacrament of growth in the Holy Spirit.

In the *Catechism* what is distinctive about the grace of confirmation is stated in comparative terms: "[I]t roots us *more deeply* in the divine filiation . . . ; it unites us *more firmly* to Christ; it increases the gifts of the Holy Spirit in us; it renders our bond with the Church *more perfect*" (CCC 1303 [emphasis added]). All this is already given in baptism, but confirmation makes it deeper, firmer, more perfect. But where does this "more" of confirmation take us?

Baptism incorporates individuals into the Church, which is the people of God and the Body of Christ (CCC 776).

> Confirmation brings with it a new factor: not only does the individual need the community, the life of the community depends on the individual's commitment and share of responsibility. Confirmation is meant to show this aspect and to enable the young Christian, endowed with the Holy Spirit, to place himself at the disposal of the missionary outreach of the Church (T. Schneider, *Zeichen der Nähe Gottes*, 117f.).

The grace of confirmation is above all a grace of sending, a commissioning for mission, for apostolate, and the strengthening for that mission. By "apostolate" the Council means every activity of the Church aimed at the sanctification of men and the ordering of them toward Christ (CCC 863): "In virtue of their union with Christ the Head, the laity have an obligation and right to the apostolate. For, incorporated into Christ's Mystical Body by baptism and strengthened with the power of the Holy Spirit in confirmation, they are entrusted with an apostolate by the Lord himself" (Decree on the Apostolate of the Laity, no. 3).

One effect of confirmation is given a special emphasis: the strengthening of Christian life for spiritual combat. The Holy Spirit at Pentecost made fearful disciples into courageous witnesses. Confirmation strengthens us with the missionary Spirit of the apostles.

28

The sacrament of sacraments

The seven sacraments form "an organic whole in which each particular sacrament has its own vital place". And the greatest and most important of all the sacraments is, of course, the Eucharist. That is why it is called "the Sacrament of sacraments": "All the other sacraments are ordered to it as to their end" (CCC 1211).

Mysterium fidei, "the mystery of faith": that is the cry of the priest after the consecration. What is the meaning of this cry? Does it mean that we are dealing here with one of the mysteries of the faith? In one sense, yes, for there are many mysteries of the faith, that is to say, realities that we can touch and grasp only in faith, such as, in the first place, the mystery of God himself, one and triune, and such as the mystery of Jesus Christ, true God and true man. "What though it baffles nature's powers of sense and sight", says Saint Thomas of the Eucharist in the *Lauda Sion*, "this faith of ours proves more than nature e'er discerned."

In another sense, it is the Eucharist itself that is the mystery of faith. In the Eucharist the Church celebrates all that she believes, her whole life.

> The whole history of salvation—the coming of Christ into the world through the Incarnation, his preaching, his sacrifice of his life on the Cross for the forgiveness of our sins, his Resurrection and exalta-

> tion—is in a way concentrated on the altar, made present and effective for men and women, who celebrate the Eucharist with one another and with the whole Church (J.-H. Nicolas, in H. Luthe, *Christusbegegnung in den Sakramenten* [1982], 294).

The Council for this reason calls the Eucharist the "source and summit of the Christian life" (CCC 1324). Here is the intersection of the two movements of the Christian life, the "descent" from God to man and the "ascent" from man to God.

The Eucharist is, first of all, God's great gift to men, the gift of his Son: "The bread of God is that which comes down from heaven, and gives life to the world. . . . I am the living bread which came down from heaven; if any one eats of this bread, he will live for ever; and the bread which I shall give for the life of the world is my flesh" (Jn 6:33, 51; CCC 1336). The Eucharist is "source and summit" of all God's gifts to us, for it "contains" Christ himself (CCC 1324), whom the Father "gave up for us all", and in whom he gives us "all things" (Rom 8:32). In the Eucharist, then, God comes to meet us. He speaks his Word to us; he reconciles us with himself through the sacrifice of love; he gives us his life through the "Bread of Life"; he sends us forth as his messengers (CCC 1332).

But the Eucharist is also the "source and summit" of man's response to God. It is the perfect prayer, because it makes present Jesus' gift of himself to his Father; it is the perfect sacrifice, because in it we insert our gifts, ourselves, into Christ's sacrifice; it is the sacrament of man's innermost union with God (CCC 1325).

29

How did Jesus celebrate the Last Supper?

Did Jesus himself institute the Eucharist? It cannot seriously be doubted that the four accounts in the New Testament of Jesus' Last Supper report essentially and exactly the same historical fact, namely, what our Lord did at supper on the night before his Passion in the upper room of a certain house in Jerusalem. However, we cannot fail to notice that there are differences in the accounts, which leave open the question: Why do only the three "Synoptic" Gospels (Saint Matthew, Saint Mark, and Saint Luke) and Saint Paul give an account of the Last Supper? Why does not Saint John? Why does he give us instead our Lord's "Eucharistic Discourse" in the synagogue at Capernaum (Jn 6) and the washing of feet and "Farewell Discourse" (Jn 13–17) on the eve of the Passion? Was Jesus' Last Supper the Jewish Passover meal (as the Synoptics say), or did it take place the day before (as John 18:28 says)?

It is certain: "From the beginning the Church has celebrated the Eucharist. The celebration of the Lord's Supper was always the center of her life!" (R. Pesch, *Wie Jesus das Abendmahl hielt* [Herder, 1977], 77). The names have changed from "the breaking of bread" (Acts 2:42) in the early Church, through "Eucharist", to "Divine Liturgy" in the Christian East and "Holy Mass" in the Latin tradition (CCC 1328–32). But what is common to all is the certainty that in this celebration we are carrying out the command of our Lord: "Do this . . . in remembrance of me" (1 Cor 11:24).

What did Jesus himself do at the Last Supper? In two places in the (Passover) meal, he did something new, something unexpected: at the beginning of the meal, when usually the blessing of bread was said, he took bread, said the blessing (perhaps in the words still used by the Jews in their prayers today), broke the bread, and gave it to his disciples with new words: "This is my body, which is given for you." At the end of the meal, when in Jewish practice the blessing over the "cup of blessing" was said, came the mysterious words: "This cup which is poured out for you is the new covenant in my blood" (Lk 22:20).

What is the meaning of these words, so familiar to us, and the actions of Jesus that accompany them? They speak of Jesus' coming death, and at the same time they make a connection with the actions and words of the Jewish Passover meal. Jesus' Passion and death will be the new Passover, which sets us free, not from slavery in Egypt, but from sin ("for the remission of sins"). Jesus' own Passover, his "passing over" to the Father through death and Resurrection, is the new and definitive "Exodus" (CCC 1340), and just as the Jewish people right up to today remember their departure out of Egypt, when they celebrate the Passover, so we celebrate the death of the Lord "until he comes" (1 Cor 11:26; CCC 1344).

Jesus' words and actions at the Last Supper do not, of course, just point toward the coming event of his Passion and Resurrection, they already anticipate it. In giving the bread and cup at the meal as his Body and Blood, he already gives the twelve disciples in the Upper Room what he obtains for the world by his Cross: redemption.

30

Continuity and change in the Mass

"It is in the liturgy itself that the Church testifies to her understanding of the Eucharist in the most profound and comprehensive way" (H. Vorgrimler, *Sakramententheologie* [Düsseldorf, 1992], 169). That is why it is important to consider the structure and form of the celebration of the Eucharist. They clearly express the meaning of the Mass.

Needless to say, the Mass has undergone many changes in the course of the centuries. How did Saint Paul celebrate the "breaking of bread" with his communities (cf. Acts 20:7–12)? What was Mass in the catacombs of Rome like? There has been a branching off into the various rites, and as a result very different forms have developed. Anyone familiar with the Byzantine liturgy of the Eastern Church knows how profoundly different it is from the Roman Catholic Mass.

And yet there is a kind of permanent basic form of the Eucharist. It has its roots in Jewish liturgy (CCC 1096) and is already evident in the second century. The *Catechism* (CCC 1345) quotes in detail the description of the Christian liturgy given in about A.D. 155 by Saint Justin Martyr. We must, of course, remember that in public Christians maintained silence about the innermost mystery of the Eucharist. Only the baptized were allowed to have access to it (the *disciplina arcani*).

Saint Justin reports that Christians came together from all directions on Sundays (CCC 1348). He is clearly describing the "Liturgy of the Word": there are readings from the writings of the apostles and prophets. He who presides then "preaches" about them. Finally, there are intercessions for all mankind. This first part closes—as is still the case today in the Eastern Church—with the kiss of peace (CCC 1349).

At the center of the celebration of the Eucharist is the prayer that gives its name to the celebration. Justin speaks of a "long thanksgiving" (*eucharistia*) spoken by the presider. This is what we now call the "Eucharistic Prayer". It is preceded by the "Presentation of the Offerings" (CCC 1350) and the collection for those in need (CCC 1351). The Eucharistic Prayer is first of all an act of praise to the Father for all the great things he has done for us, above all for the gift of his Son, for his death and Resurrection. That is the content of what we call the "Preface" (CCC 1352).

In Jewish prayer the memorial of the mighty deeds of God was already not a mere calling to mind but a true making present. Christ's Passion, death, and Resurrection become present in the memorial (CCC 1357). Through the power of Christ's words ("This is my Body . . .") and the working of the Holy Spirit, the sacrifice of Christ, Christ himself, indeed, becomes present under the species of bread and wine (CCC 1353). The celebration is completed with the "Supper of the Lord", in the receiving of the bread and wine that have been "made Eucharist", the Body and Blood of Christ (CCC 1355).

However much may have changed, these essential elements remain down the centuries the "Mass of all times" (CCC 1356).

31

The Sacrifice of the Mass

The phrase "Sacrifice of the Mass" has somewhat fallen out of use. And yet it expresses something essential about the meaning of the Eucharist, which we must not be allowed to forget. What does "sacrifice" mean here? The Council says this: "At the Last Supper, on the night he was betrayed, our Savior instituted the Eucharistic sacrifice of his Body and Blood. This he did in order to perpetuate the sacrifice of the cross throughout the ages until he should come again, and so to entrust to his beloved Spouse, the Church, a memorial of his death and resurrection" (CCC 1323).

Three statements in particular need to be emphasized here: (1) Jesus' death on the Cross was a sacrifice, as was the celebration instituted by him at the Last Supper; (2) the two are connected: through the Eucharistic Sacrifice the sacrifice of the Cross is perpetuated; (3) this perpetuation takes place in the form of a "memorial".

Our Lord Jesus Christ lived his whole life on earth as an offering to the Father (CCC 606). His life and suffering express his mission "to serve and to give his life as a ransom for many" (Mk 10:45; CCC 608). If we are to understand and to be able to celebrate the Mass as a sacrifice, then we have to remember that Christ shed his blood for us and for all men "for the forgiveness of sins". "There is not, never has been, and never will be a single human being for whom Christ did not suffer" (CCC 605). The Cross of Jesus is the perfect, unique sacrifice. It is not first of all a human effort to get God to be merciful but, rather, the gift of the Father to us: He shows us his reconciling love when Christ "takes away" the whole burden of the No of sin through the Yes of his love.

Our Lord wanted what he accomplished "once and for all" (CCC 616) "[to be perpetuated] throughout the ages until he should come again". To this end, on the night before he died, he instituted the sacrifice that we celebrate today in obedience to his command. In what sense is the Eucharist a sacrifice? First, because it is the memorial of the one sacrifice of Christ: "Do this in remembrance of me" (1 Cor 11:24). "Memorial" here does not mean mere "recollection", "commemoration", but "making present" (CCC 1363): in the Eucharist, when we proclaim and thus remember Christ's death and Resurrection, they are "re-presented", that is, shown forth and made present (CCC 1366).

The sacrifice of Christ is not repeated. It took place once and for all, valid for all times. But in the celebration of the Eucharist it is made present and in a certain way becomes efficacious for us, is given to us. That is why the Council says, in the words of an ancient liturgical text: "As often as the sacrifice of the Cross by which 'Christ our Pasch has been sacrificed' is celebrated on the altar, the work of our redemption is carried out" (CCC 1364). When we ponder these words in our hearts, how precious does the gift of the Eucharist appear to us!

32

The Mass—sacrifice of Christ and sacrifice of the Church

The prophet Malachi foretold: "From the rising of the sun to its setting my name is great among the nations, and in every place incense is offered to my name, and a pure offering" (Mal 1:11). From earliest times Christian authors have read these words as a promise of the Eucharist, which is offered all over the earth by those of all nations who have converted to Christ. The Council of Trent (1562) gives the same teaching: "This is that pure offering which cannot be defiled by any unworthiness or wickedness in those who offer it." The Third Eucharistic Prayer takes up Malachi's prophecy once more: "You never cease to gather a people to yourself, so that from the rising of the sun to its setting a pure offering may be made to your name."

What does it mean to say that, though the sacrifice is always one and the same, it is offered up all over the world? "One Sacrifice and Many Masses"—that was the title of a book by Karl Rahner. The Council of Trent gives us this explanation: "In this divine sacrifice which is celebrated in the Mass, the same Christ who offered himself once in a bloody manner on the altar of the Cross is contained and is offered in an unbloody manner. . . . [For] the victim is one and the same: the same now offers through the ministry of priests, who then offered himself on the cross; only the manner of offering is different" (CCC 1367).

What does it mean for the Church, for us, to celebrate the sacrifice of Christ? We have the ancient custom of offering Mass for the living or the dead, for the special intentions of the Church, of individuals, and society, and to give for that purpose a certain sum of money, a "Mass stipend". Many people object to this practice, but they forget that in poor countries the Mass stipend is one of the few ways by which the priest can support himself. True, Mass can be neither bought nor sold, but the financial offering (the collection plate, the Mass stipend) can be an expression of our "investment" of ourselves, our whole life, all our cares and concerns, in the one sacrifice of Christ. We can unite ourselves with his offering of his life to the Father for the salvation of all mankind and, through our visible sacrificial contribution, express the fact that we are offering ourselves with Christ "on the altar of our hearts".

The Eucharist is the sacrifice of the Church, because the Church is "the Body of Christ" (CCC 1368): he for us, we with him, Head and members. His self-offering takes place for us, and we are able to unite our life, all that we do and suffer, to him. In the liturgical action this participation is symbolized by the mixing of a drop of water with the wine in the chalice. "By the mystery of this water and wine may we come to share in the divinity of Christ, who humbled himself to share in our humanity." Our "little offering" is made one with the great and unique sacrifice of Christ.

33

The presence of Christ in the Eucharist

In a catechetical discourse of the early Church we read: "Do not look upon the bread and wine as something ordinary, for, by the Lord's own words, they are his Body and Blood. Even though perception suggests this to you, let faith grant you certainty. Do not judge the matter by taste! Be firmly convinced by faith that you have become worthy of the Body and Blood of Christ!" (Saint Cyril of Jerusalem, *Mystagogical Catecheses* 4, 6). And Saint Ambrose says to the newly baptized: "Before the consecration it was not the Body of Christ, but after the consecration, I assure you, it is the Body of Christ" (*On the Sacraments* 4, 16).

The presence of Christ in the Eucharist is unique among the different modes of his presence (CCC 1373). During his sermons and catechetical instructions, the Curé of Ars used to turn time and again toward the tabernacle and cry out: "He is there!" Those simple words of faith express far better than the efforts of theology what is special about this presence of the Lord. The Council of Trent says that he is "truly, really, and substantially" present (CCC 1374). Christ is present with his Body and Blood, divinity and humanity, with his whole self-oblation, with his death and his Resurrection. He himself is really present, not just a part of him, not a mere symbol of his presence, but he himself, not, of course, in his earthly appearance but "under the appearances of bread and wine", in a "sacramental way", that is to say, in a way that is hidden from the senses and yet real and efficacious. This mode of his presence "cannot be apprehended by the senses, but only by faith" (Saint Thomas Aquinas, CCC 1381).

Only in faith can we understand what happens when Christ brings about his presence in the Eucharist: through the change of bread and wine into his Body and Blood. Just as the sacramental presence of Christ is unique, so is this change. All the changes accessible to our human observation change something that continues to exist: metal is heated, water frozen, the artist shapes his material, human beings change and yet remain themselves. Here it is different: bread and wine do not change their appearance, their taste, their properties. It is their *substance* that is changed: "This is my Body", "This is my Blood." Under the appearances that remain, Christ himself has become present. The Fathers compare this event to creation "out of nothing" (CCC 1375, 298). God's power alone can do such a thing. The words of Christ, spoken by the priest, have an effect that no human power can have: "The Holy Spirit comes upon them and accomplishes what surpasses every word and thought" (Saint John Damascene, CCC 1106).

The genuflections that we make after the consecration, before Communion, and in front of the tabernacle are justified only when they are directed toward him who "is there", in our midst, under the very humble appearance of bread.

34

Eucharistic Communion

The book of Exodus describes a mysterious scene. Moses communicates to the people the words of the covenant, the commandments of God. Then he sets up an altar, and animals are offered up in sacrifice. He sprinkles the altar and the people with the blood of the beasts: "Behold the blood of the covenant. . . ." Finally, he climbs the mountain with the elders: "[T]hey beheld the God, and ate and drank" (Ex 24:1–11).

Sacrifice and meal belong together: the sacrifice signifies thanksgiving and reconciliation; it restores communion between man and God (CCC 2099). The sprinkling with blood symbolizes this renewed communion of life, while the meal sets a seal upon it. Communion at the altar flows into communion in the meal. This is something the Eucharist has in common not only with the Old Testament but with many other religions (CCC 28). And yet it is incomparable: the sacrifice offered here is as unique as the meal that follows from it: Christ himself is the offering, the offerer, and the food. He reconciles us with the Father, and he gives himself to us for food, as the Father's gift.

The primary purpose of Holy Communion is, therefore, intimate communion with Christ: "He who eats my flesh and drinks my blood abides in me, and I in him" (Jn

6:56). Of course, union with Christ requires faith if it is to grow and become deeper. The "Amen" with which we respond to "The Body of Christ" is meant to be an expression of faith: "Yes, so it is; yes, I believe!" (CCC 1064).

It is the usual practice now—and in itself this is a good thing (CCC 1388)—that many, in fact most, of the faithful go to Communion. All the more important, then, is our preparation beforehand, something that years ago, when Communion was infrequent, was often carried out very thoughtfully and carefully. After all, we receive not just "consecrated bread" but the very One who calls himself "the living bread" (Jn 6:51). That is why the priest's silent prayers of preparation should be prayed (silently) with him by all of us, to make ourselves realize who it is we are receiving and to confess in faith: "Lord, I am not worthy" (CCC 1386). Reverence for the sacred presence of our Lord should be expressed in demeanor and gestures when we receive Holy Communion (CCC 1387). It will move us to repentance and conversion when we discover our sinfulness (CCC 208). The sacrament of penance is the door through which Christ's healing mercy approaches us anew.

But Holy Communion also signifies our communion with one another: "Because there is one bread, we who are many are one body, for we all partake of the one bread" (1 Cor 10:17). From many grains comes the one loaf, and from many believers comes the one Body of Christ (CCC 1396). Communion is, therefore, authentic, incurring not "judgment" (1 Cor 11:29), only when it is also a communion of sharing, especially with those who are the very poorest of Christ's brethren (CCC 1397): "Be then a member of the Body of Christ that your *Amen* may be true" (Saint Augustine; CCC 1396).

35

Eucharistic adoration

"The Catholic Church has always offered and still offers to the sacrament of the Eucharist the cult of adoration, not only during Mass, but also outside of it" (CCC 1378). To go from Christ's presence in the eucharistic celebration of the community to adoration of Christ under the sacramental species of bread is a step that many Catholics today find it hard to take. It is no doubt incomprehensible to most Protestant Christians and is regarded by Eastern Orthodox Christians as a Catholic speciality. Many people think it would be best if this form of piety, a product of history, should now be allowed to disappear.

On the other hand, we find that much of the living renewal in the Church today has a strong attachment to eucharistic adoration. Many personal testimonies could be cited. Let me mention just one, a Jewish convert, the late Sister Miriam Prager of the Benedictine Abbey of Saint Gabriel (*Das Buch meines Lebens* [Graz, 1981], 35f.). Sister Miriam received her call to baptism, to faith in Christ, in a chapel at the very moment of Benediction of the Blessed Sacrament, the meaning of which she knew nothing. Something similar happened to André Frossard when by chance he visited the chapel of perpetual adoration in the rue d'Ulm in Paris (cf. *Gott existiert: Ich bin ihm begegnet* [Freiburg, 1974]).

We hear two main objections to eucharistic adoration: first, that our Lord said only "Take and eat"; and second, that we are dealing here with a form of piety that developed very late in history. With regard to this second objection, we should remember that much of what is familiar to us in liturgy and piety today developed only gradually. That does not mean it has to be a false or inauthentic development. It was precisely the deepening of faith in the eucharistic presence of our Lord that led to new forms of devotion to the Blessed Sacrament, from the Corpus Christi procession to greater prominence for the tabernacle, exposition of the Blessed Sacrament, and silent adoration. This deepening of devotion in the course of history is not an aberration.

But the deepest reason for eucharistic adoration is to be found in the species of the Sacrament itself. True, bread is for eating, and Jesus commanded his disciples to eat the bread that had become his Body. But if we thought more deeply about what the species of bread signifies, then we would grasp the full eucharistic meaning of adoration. In his Eucharistic Discourse at Capernaum, our Lord calls himself "the bread of life" (Jn 6:35). His whole life is to be "bread from heaven", the bread that gives life by giving itself. The presence of Jesus under the species of bread signifies the deepest meaning of his mission: he is and he remains among us as the bread broken for us and given to us, our food, our "staff of life" (CCC 1380). In our silent adoration of the eucharistic bread, his mission should imprint itself upon our life: to become, like him, bread "for the life of the world".

36

Ecumenism at the Lord's Supper?

"The desire to recover the unity of all Christians is a gift of Christ and a call of the Holy Spirit" (CCC 820). Nowhere does the lack of unity become more painful, nowhere do we become more vividly aware of the urgency of unity than at the "Lord's Supper". That is why there is a longing on the part of many Christians for full unity, sealed and strengthened by "common participation in the table of the Lord" (CCC 1398). Many people insist that this unity should be simply anticipated by requesting or demanding intercommunion before the communion of the Churches has been restored. But if true unity is to be furthered, progress toward that goal should be made in truth and in love, so that new rifts do not increase our disunity.

"Baptism constitutes the foundation of communion among all Christians" (CCC 1271). Anyone who is not baptized cannot share in the Lord's Supper. No one is excluded from the love of Christians, but only someone who has received the "washing of regeneration" can share in fellowship with them at the table of the Lord. But baptism is only the beginning, for it "seeks for the attainment of the fullness of life in Christ" (*Directory for the Application of Principles and Norms on Ecumenism*, no. 92), and thus for the common reception of Christ in the Eucharist.

Of course, separated Christians hold some sharply differing views about the meaning and importance of the Lord's Supper. These differences concern first and foremost the meaning of the priesthood, the Sacrifice of the Mass, and the Real Presence of Christ in the Eucharist (CCC 1400). For Holy Communion to be true and fruitful, it must not be isolated from the totality of the eucharistic celebration.

There is now a quite simple and illuminating criterion for deciding whether a common reception of Holy Communion corresponds to the truth. When someone receives the Eucharist, he hears the words "The Body of Christ" and gives the response "Amen", "Yes, it is, I firmly believe it be so!" This Amen is preceded by the communal "Amen" at the end of the Eucharistic Prayer, after the words "Through him, with him, in him". If the "Amen" to "The Body of Christ" is to ring true, then it must be in harmony with the "Amen" to the Eucharistic Prayer, through which the eucharistic Body of Christ has become present.

The "Amen" signifies assent to the offering of the sacrifice "in union with our Pope and our bishop", to fellowship with Mary and all the saints, "on whose intercession we rely", to prayer for "our departed brothers and sisters", and above all to the fact that bread and wine, by the power of the Holy Spirit and the words of Christ, spoken by the priest, "become for us the Body and Blood of [God's] Son, our Lord Jesus Christ".

Anyone who can give his Yes and Amen to these things is affirming the Eucharist as it is understood by the Catholic Church. He is saying Yes to the communion of this Catholic Church. His Yes and Amen to the fruit of this Eucharistic Prayer, the eucharistic Body of Christ, will also then be true. There are special situations in which Christians not in full communion with the Catholic Church can receive the Eucharist (CCC 1401). The prerequisite for this will always be that they can say the twofold "Amen" with an upright heart.

37

The pledge of future glory

In the celebration of the Eucharist, the eyes of the faithful turn not just back to the beginning, to the room of the Last Supper, to the night when our Lord instituted and entrusted to his Church the memorial of his Passion and Resurrection. At the Last Supper, our Lord himself looked into the future, not only to the time when his disciples would "do this in memory" of him, as he had commanded them to do, but beyond that to "the day when [he] would drink [this fruit of the vine] new in [his] Father's Kingdom" (Mt 26:29; CCC 1403).

In the Eucharist not only do Jesus' death and Resurrection become present, so too does his coming again in glory. His coming in the sacrament anticipates his future coming (CCC 331, 671). he really and truly comes, even though his presence is veiled and his coming hidden (CCC 1404).

Nowadays our sense of this orientation of the eucharistic celebration to the coming glory of Christ is often underdeveloped. And yet it is one of the essential aspects of the Eucharist that it is a "pledge of future glory", that in the Eucharist heaven already comes down to earth, and the earthly Church opens herself upward to her heavenly home. Here are some helpful suggestions for awakening a sense of this truth:

The early Church had a lively awareness of the "eschatological" dimension of the Church. Jews, wherever they were, always said their prayers turning toward Jerusalem, but Christians, from very early on, prayed toward the east, the direction of the rising sun, which for them was the symbol of the Second Coming of Christ. Synagogues were built facing Jerusalem, but churches toward the east. That is where the word "orientation" comes from: it means "east-ing". Today we have "lost our orientation". We are no longer so vividly aware that in the celebration of the Eucharist we encounter Christ the Lord, who is coming again. For centuries priest and people prayed together facing east. This idea is suggested anew by the Second Vatican Council's teaching that the Church is a pilgrim people, a people whose goal is the Kingdom of God in its final perfection. As they pray and celebrate the Eucharist, they are on their way toward that destination. It is a beautiful expression of this common pilgrimage when priest and faithful together, as they "go to meet Christ", pray facing east. The "old" direction for the celebration of Mass was not a turning away from the faithful by the priest but a common turning toward the Lord by priest and faithful together. It is good not to forget this form of celebration.

But the usual form of celebration today, "turned toward the people", can also remind us of the coming of the Lord. After all, the Council teaches us that the priest acts "in the person of Christ" (*in persona Christi*). Through the sacrament of ordination the priest in the celebration of the Eucharist represents Christ, who in his Word and sacrament comes to meet the faithful.

So both directions for the celebration have justification and a profound meaning.

What really matters is that we become aware in a new and deeper way that in the celebration of the Eucharist all the angels and saints in the glory of heaven are celebrating with us, because Christ himself comes to be in our midst. The dignity and solemnity of liturgical vestments are a sign and expression of this glory that has been bestowed upon us.

So it is not surprising that since the time of the apostles, during the celebration of the Eucharist, the great longing breaks out in a cry of prayer: *Maranatha* (1 Cor 16:22), "Come, Lord Jesus" (Rev 22:20).

38

Healing through the sacraments

The *Catechism* divides the seven sacraments into three groups: the three "sacraments of Christian initiation" (baptism, confirmation, Eucharist), the two "sacraments of healing" (penance and the anointing of the sick), and the "sacraments at the service of communion" (orders and marriage). This division has been criticized, not without some justification, as somewhat artificial. Are not all the sacraments at the service of communion? True, First Communion is one of the "sacraments of initiation", but does that apply to the regular communal celebration of the Eucharist? And, above all, we hear the objection that all the sacraments have a healing effect.

Father Michael Marsch, O.P., has written a book, based on his rich experience as priest and psychotherapist, with the title *Heilung durch die Sakramente* (Healing through the sacraments) (Styria, 1987). He points out that catechesis on the sacraments in the early Church liked to refer to the healing miracles of Jesus. In the *Catechism*, too, the healing effect of the sacraments is presented through the image of the healing of the woman with the flow of blood. This woman, who had been ill for many years, was healed through "the power that came forth from him" when she touched the robe of our Lord (cf. the picture at the beginning of part 2). The sacraments of the Church continue now what Christ did during his earthly life. Through the sacraments, Christ himself touches, strengthens, heals us. The sacraments are, so to speak, the earthly hands of the heavenly, risen Lord. What he touches is healed.

Christ does not heal by simply taking away the symptoms of the illness. His healing goes into the depths. As he said to the paralytic: "My son, your sins are forgiven" (Mk 2:5). Christ heals the whole man. His healing begins at the root of all that is unhealthy: the sin that separates us from God, the source of life (CCC 1421). That is why the healing element of the forgiveness of sins is part of every sacrament. We become really healthy only when we are reconciled with God, united with Christ, and filled with the Holy Spirit. Then pain and sickness can also have a positive "salutary" effect. "How mild are the troubles of this world, when we have the Holy Spirit!", said the Curé of Ars.

The more we recognize in faith the Church herself as the sacrament of God's love, the more the healing dimension of the sacraments will open itself up to us. She is healing fellowship, loving Mother, who dispenses the "medicine" of Christ to us. As Father Marsch says: "The sacraments are not meant to make us think the world is healed. They are neither drugs nor magic. Jesus did not promise us a rose garden. But through encounter with the Savior, the sacraments can make a decisive contribution to the healing of the individual in an ever more incurable world." In what follows, we shall speak of the healing power of two sacraments in particular: the sacrament of penance and the sacrament of the anointing of the sick.

39

Who can forgive sins?

"Who can forgive sins but God alone?" (Mk 2:7). This question of the scribes goes to the very heart of what sin is: No to God. That is why God alone can forgive that No (CCC 1441).

Now experience shows that the recognition of sin as sin cannot be taken for granted. We acknowledge our faults, notice our imperfections, regret our mistakes, feel sorry for hurting people. But what does this have to do with God? It seems perfectly reasonable that we need reconciliation, that we should forgive one another. But it is hard to imagine how we can "offend God" (CCC 1440). It is less difficult for us to see the social dimension of sin than the reference of sin to God. And yet the Psalmist prays: "Against you, you alone, have I sinned" (Ps 51:6; CCC 1850).

At the beginning of the Gospel comes the call to conversion, to repentance (Mk 1:15; CCC 1427). Conversion is about two things that are inseparable: our relationship with God and our attitude toward our neighbor. New life according to the gospel is summed up in the twofold commandment of love of God and love of neighbor. And yet we must observe the proper order: we must love God "with all our heart, and with all our soul, and with all our mind, and with all our strength" (Mk 12:30), and we must love our neighbor "as ourself" (Mk 12:31).

"Sin", too, then, is always two things: No to the love of God and a wounding of love of neighbor. And yet we become conscious of *sin* only to the extent that we encounter the love of God. That is the only explanation for the fact that it is precisely the saints who have such an acute awareness of sin: the more God's love takes hold of them, the greater the pain they feel for having offended that love.

We cannot "offend" God in the way that we inflict insults on one another. But the sorrow of repentance can move us to see that we have responded so little to God's love, that we have not loved him "with all our heart". And this sorrow can also take hold of us when we realize our lack of love for our neighbor, for whom God has such boundless love. In this sense, sin is always first of all to do with God and can be forgiven by him alone.

The bringing of this forgiveness is the special mission of Jesus. His very name means "he will save his people from their sins" (Mt 1:21). And at the end of his earthly journey he says: "This is my Blood, . . . which is poured out for many for the forgiveness of sins" (Mt 26:28). Because Jesus is the Son of God, he can say of himself: "The Son of Man has authority on earth to forgive sins" (Mt 9:6; CCC 1441). He does something still greater (cf. Jn 14:12): he has entrusted his disciples with this authority that belongs to God alone, so that in his name they may exercise the "ministry of reconciliation" (2 Cor 5:18) and forgive sins (cf. Jn 20:21–23).

It is one of the greatest and most beautiful things that men can do in the power of Jesus: to utter efficaciously the healing words, "I absolve you from all your sins."

40

Confession—the forgotten sacrament?

The first gift of the risen Lord to his disciples was peace and joy: "Peace be with you!" That is how he greeted them in the Upper Room: "Then the disciples were glad when they saw the Lord" (Jn 20:19–20). But peace and joy are not meant for them alone. That is why the Lord sends them, "As the Father has sent me, even so I send you" (Jn 20:21), and equips them for the task: "Receive the Holy Spirit. If you forgive the sins of any, they are forgiven; if you retain the sins of any, they are retained" (Jn 20:22–23). How do the apostles, how does the Church, see this commission from our Lord (CCC 976)?

The *Catechism* says this:

> Christ has willed that in her prayer and life and action his whole Church should be the sign and instrument of the forgiveness and reconciliation that he acquired for us at the price of his blood. But he entrusted the exercise of the power of absolution to the apostolic ministry. . . . The apostle is sent out "on behalf of Christ" with "God making his appeal" through him and pleading: "Be reconciled to God" (2 Cor 5:20) (CCC 1442).

In the course of the centuries the outward form of this "ministry of reconciliation" (2 Cor 5:18) has undergone great changes. For Christians who have committed particularly grave sins after baptism, Saint Paul recognizes the need for the severe punishment of expulsion, so that the man concerned may at least "be saved in the day of the Lord Jesus" (1 Cor 5:5). To a large extent the early Church followed this rigorous penitential practice and for grave public sins imposed public penance, sometimes lifelong (CCC 1447). This penance, which included exclusion from eucharistic Communion, was regarded as "the second plank [of salvation] after the shipwreck which is the loss of grace" (CCC 1446).

This rigorous discipline proved, in so many different ways, to be humanly and pastorally intolerable, and so, from the early Middle Ages onward, especially under the influence of the Irish monks, a new form of "private penance", or "auricular confession", developed, with the possibility of receiving absolution not just at the end of the time of penance but immediately after the confession of sins in the presence of the priest. Thus arose our present form of confession, which has remained essentially the same for more than a thousand years (CCC 1448).

Are we again today on the threshold of another radical change? Hardly any other sacrament has suffered such decline in recent years. Has the consciousness of sin faded away? Have there been too many negative experiences of confession? Is the shortage of priests having an effect here, too? On the other hand, the problem of unrecognized and unrepented sin is a heavy, crushing burden that does damage to the life of the individual and of the community (CCC 386).

Wherever in the Church today there are new signs of life, there is a rediscovery of the sacrament of penance.

Then what the disciples experienced on the evening of Easter Day takes place anew: the risen Lord, through his Holy Spirit, bestows reconciliation and peace.

41

Contrition and confession

There are three steps in the sacrament of penance: contrition, confession of sins, and satisfaction. If any one of these is missing, then conversion has not really been accomplished, and the sacrament cannot bear its fruit.

But what is contrition? The philosopher Max Scheler wrote some wonderfully illuminating things about the phenomenon in his book *Reue und Wiedergeburt* [Repentance and regeneration]. He shows first of all how many obstacles confront a right understanding of contrition today. Take, for example, this attitude: "Why be contrite about what can't be changed? What's done is done! Don't have regrets, better to move on! Contrition is just fear of punishment, fear of being 'found out'; it is the depression you feel after you have done something; it is the attempt to ease a troubled conscience through self-punishment." These and similar opinions about contrition are widespread. But they can also be viewed as caricatures of genuine contrition. What does genuine contrition look like?

The Council of Trent mentions three elements. Contrition is "sorrow of soul and detestation for the sin committed, together with the resolution not to sin again" (CCC 1451). The path to repentance can be a long one. To begin with, there may be just a vague feeling, a discomforting recollection of something not being as it should be. This situation becomes clearer, when, suddenly or gradually, I painfully realize that I did something wrong. "How could it happen, to me of all people?" This question makes a breach in the walls of our pride, our exaggerated sense of our own importance. Now the act I committed—or omitted to do—can be seen for what it is: the evil I did or the good I neglected to do. And the consequences of this are sorrow in the heart and abhorrence for the evil we have done.

Here we see how contrition can lead to "regeneration". I perceive and acknowledge my guilt (which in the moment of the act I may not have noticed or seen). I recognize that I could, I should, have acted differently. Here lies a great hope. The good that I neglected to do attracts me. I can now pledge myself to it anew, at least I can yearn for it. Contrition opens up a new future for me.

This kind of perception, which converts the heart, is always a gift of God, a prompting of the Holy Spirit (CCC 1453). Contrition is "perfect" when it is sorrow for having offended love (CCC 1452). It is called "imperfect" when it is motivated more by fear of punishment.

Contrition moves us to confession, not just to any kind of confession to anybody, but to the naming and voicing of the sin for which one has contrition. Only in confession do I take responsibility for my sins and overcome them, thereby opening myself to reconciliation (CCC 1455).

But why do we have to make our confession to a priest? "[I]f the sick person is too ashamed to show his wound to the doctor, the medicine cannot heal what it does not know" (Saint Jerome, CCC 1456). In confession I show the priest even the hidden wounds of my sins, so that he can heal them with Christ's forgiveness.

42

The different forms of penance, confessors, spiritual direction

People go to confession much less often than they used to. And yet everywhere people are looking for someone to support and help them spiritually and psychologically. Many look for this in their doctor or therapist. Personal confession to a priest and the "spiritual direction" that he can offer seem to be asked for less and less. Is that really so? There are many signs to make us hopeful that it is not so. Something new is developing. An ancient treasure, tried and tested, is being rediscovered.

This is happening, first of all, in the different forms of penance. "Without being strictly necessary, confession of everyday faults (venial sins) is nevertheless strongly recommended by the Church" (CCC 1458). There are many different forms of penance through which we can obtain forgiveness for our "venial" sins. Fasting, prayer, and almsgiving are the three cited in Scripture (CCC 1434). "Taking up one's cross each day and following Jesus is the surest way of penance" (CCC 1435). The crucial thing is our daily readiness for conversion and active love, "since love covers a multitude of sins" (1 Pet 4:8).

And this is why regular personal confession (so-called "confession of devotion") makes sense. It refines the conscience and deepens our union with Christ. "By receiving more frequently through this sacrament the gift of the Father's mercy, we are spurred to be merciful as he is merciful" (CCC 1458).

The communal celebration of penance is not in contradiction with this. Sin wounds communion, and so penance and conversion always have a communitarian character (CCC 1429, 1443). Penance services can make us aware of this truth and can lead to both personal repentance and communal supplication for the forgiveness of sins (CCC 1482). "General absolution" from the priest is, of course, restricted to situations of grave necessity. This is not an arbitrary limitation imposed by the Church. There are good reasons for it: Christ never carried out collective healings. He addresses each sinner personally. "He is the physician tending each one of the sick" (CCC 1484). Absolution, too, is personal: "I absolve *you* . . ." [Latin *te*, singular].

"Hearing confessions": there is no task in the life of a priest in which he experiences so profoundly what it means to carry out the ministry of the Good Shepherd. If this ministry is missing, then so, too, is a wellspring of life for priestly existence. Here the priest realizes that he has the privilege of exercising the ministry of the Good Samaritan, that he really can be an instrument of the forgiving love of God (CCC 1465). This makes it all the more important for the penitent to be able to recognize in the priest a servant of the mercy of Christ. But at the same time he must also believe that in the priest to whom he confesses and who gives him absolution he really does encounter Christ.

"Spiritual direction" is not tied to the sacrament of penance. It presupposes the gift of "discernment of spirits" (CCC 2690). Here a wide field of spiritual ministry opens up for lay people, both men and women.

43

The anointing of the sick

In the German-speaking world, when someone is ill, we occasionally speak of *Heimsuchung*. This lovely old word means two things: that here is a trial, a form of suffering, but also that behind the trial stands Someone who is addressing us, who is knocking on the door of our heart and, yes, is "calling us home".

Sickness and suffering are part of human life, and yet they ought not to be part of human life. We defend ourselves against them, fight them, try to contain and relieve them, and yet we have to accept them, to say Yes to them. Every illness reminds us that death is waiting for us (CCC 1500).

Our dealings with sickness and death have undergone far-reaching changes in both Church and society. In rural areas I have met people who still know by heart the long prayers for the dying. Dying used to be surrounded with rites and prayers. Nowadays it usually leaves us speechless and helpless. It has been pushed into the anonymity of the hospital, ousted from life. And yet slowly but surely we are learning anew that dying is the final and essential step that we take in life. A welcome sign of this is the "hospice movement".

The liturgical accompaniment of sickness and death has also radically changed. In the old days the priest was regarded as the "angel of death" at a sickbed. People tried to postpone extreme unction as late as possible, in fact, till after the sick person had died. That is why the Council introduced a reform that is still going on: the sacrament is again called "the anointing of the sick", and it is meant for the sick and not only for the dying (CCC 1499).

The model for the sacrament is the healing work of Jesus, which makes his compassion with all human suffering "tangible". Jesus takes his disciples into this "ministry of compassion and healing" (CCC 1506): "Heal the sick . . . [The Twelve] went out . . . and anointed with oil many that were sick and healed them" (Mt 10:8; Mk 6:12–13).

From the beginning, Christians have held care for the sick in high esteem (CCC 1509). In the sick we serve Christ himself (Mt 25:36). Prayer for the sick is part of this ministry. We are all called to it and should do it consciously and deliberately. In cases of grave illness, when "anyone of the faithful begins to be in danger of death from sickness or old age" (as the Council says), then the time has come for anointing of the sick by the priest (CCC 1514–16).

The *Catechism* mentions three effects of this sacrament: (1) strengthening by the Holy Spirit in the distress of illness; (2) the grace to unite one's own suffering with the Passion of Christ (the sick person is "in a certain way . . . consecrated" to work for the salvation of men through his suffering with Christ); (3) a contribution, through suffering borne in faith, "to the good of all men" (CCC 1520–22). We all too easily forget that, by the grace of Christ, being sick is a hidden but profoundly efficacious apostolate. Mother Teresa insisted that every one of her sisters have "behind her" someone who, by offering up his illness, would help the sister to carry out her apostolate.

44

The sacrament of holy orders

"Holy Orders is the sacrament through which the mission entrusted by Christ to his apostles continues to be exercised in the Church until the end of time: thus it is the sacrament of apostolic ministry" (CCC 1536). This brief definition of the sacrament of holy orders assumes something that frequently these days cannot be taken for granted. Take, for example this line of questioning: "Jesus called and sent out the apostles. But did he want priests and bishops? Did he want the sacrament of holy orders? Don't all Christians carry on Christ's mission? What's the point of priests? What's the point of bishops? What's the point of 'office' in the Church? Isn't 'hierarchy' much more a work of man than something instituted by Christ?"

These questions have been hotly debated by Christians at least since the Reformation in the sixteenth century. And so they are again today, with people talking about "the official Church", as if ordained office were something alien to the Church.

In the New Covenant there is only one priest, Jesus Christ, the only "mediator between God and men" (1 Tim 2:5), and his sacrifice is unique, offered once for all on the Cross for the whole of mankind. How, then, can there be priests, a special sacrament of ordination? Is this not an aberration, a break with the original tradition? The *Catechism* offers a helpful analogy:

"The redemptive sacrifice of Christ is unique, accomplished once for all; yet it is made present in the Eucharistic sacrifice of the Church. The same is true of the one priesthood of Christ; it is made present through the ministerial priesthood without diminishing the uniqueness of Christ's priesthood" (CCC 1545). Some words of Saint Thomas are quoted to explain it even more clearly: "Only Christ is the true priest, the others being only his ministers."

Unfortunately, in German we use the word *Amt*, "office", which leads to the totally misleading phrase "official Church" and reminds people of the offices and authorities of our secular society. But in the original Latin of the Council the phrase always used is "ministerial priesthood" (*sacerdotium ministeriale*). Priestly ministry derives its mission, its meaning, its efficacy from Christ (CCC 1551). That is the only thing that makes sense of the priest saying "This is my Body", "This is my Blood." He is not telling a story from the past. He is speaking and acting "in the person of Christ the Head", as the Council says (CCC 1548).

The priest also prays and celebrates the liturgy "in the name of the whole Church", not as if he were the elected "delegate of the community", but because he represents Christ, who is "the Head of the Body, the Church" and who offers himself to God the Father with and for us all, making intercession for us with God (CCC 1553).

Is it not asking far too much of weak and sinful men that they should "represent Christ"? But that is why ordination is a sacrament: it is not a human accomplishment, but a gift of God, conferred through human hands and hearts.

45

The ministry of bishops

Bishops, priests, deacons: the Church's ordained ministry has been handed down to us in these three degrees. This is how it has been exercised, says the Council, "even from ancient times" (CCC 1554). Our next three chapters will speak of these three forms of ordained ministry: where they come from, how they are connected, and what they mean.

The outward form of the episcopal office has changed in many ways in the course of the centuries, but its essential task remains the same until the Lord returns.

> The divine mission which Christ entrusted to the apostles will last to the end of the world (cf. Mt 28:20), for the gospel, which they are to teach, is for every age the source of all life in the Church. For this reason the apostles took care . . . to appoint successors. They did not just have helpers in their ministry, but, so that the mission assigned to them might continue after their death, they handed on to their immediate successors, as a kind of testament, the task of completing and strengthening the work that they had begun. . . . They therefore appointed such men, and gave them the order that, likewise on their death, other tried and tested men should take over their ministry.

That is how the Council (*Lumen gentium*, no. 20) describes the transition from the apostles to their successors, the bishops. This teaching is supported by our earliest documents, which testify to this transition. Most important of all, apart from the letters of Saint Paul and the Acts of the Apostles, is the letter of Saint Clement of Rome, the third successor of Saint Peter, to the community in Corinth (c. A.D. 96). In the letters of the martyr bishop Saint Ignatius of Antioch (c. A.D. 110), we find the Church's ordained ministry already structured in three degrees: "Let everyone revere the deacons as Jesus Christ, the bishop as the image of the Father, and the presbyters as the senate of God and the assembly of the apostles. For without them one cannot speak of the Church" (CCC 1554). Some time later (c. A.D. 180) Saint Irenaeus is already telling us about the lists of bishops of the particular Churches founded by the apostles, and he lists by name the successors of Saint Peter in Rome right up to his own day.

Thus, with impressive continuity, the "apostolic succession" has endured from the Church's beginning to today. It draws its inner strength and life from the bestowal of the grace of the sacrament. To fulfill their mission, the apostles received "a special outpouring of the Holy Spirit". "[B]y the imposition of hands they passed on to their auxiliaries the gift of the Spirit (cf. 1 Tim 4:14; 2 Tim 1:6–7), which is transmitted down to our day through episcopal consecration" (CCC 1556). The Council teaches (one of its few explicit dogmatic teachings) that "*the fullness of the sacrament of Holy Orders* is conferred by episcopal consecration" (CCC 1557). And so the bishops, regardless of their human strengths and weaknesses, really are the successors of the apostles.

46

The ministry of priests

Are not all the baptized priests? Is not the people of God as a whole "a royal priesthood" (1 Pet 2:9)? Why, then, is there is a special sacrament of priestly ordination? The question is not without point. It concerns our communities and our families and, in a very personal way, individuals. Do we want priests? Do we pray for them? Are we glad when a young man discovers he has a vocation to the priesthood? Do we promote vocations to the priesthood?

There is a passage in the Council's Dogmatic Constitution on the Church that has been a constant cause of discussion: "Although the common priesthood of the faithful and the ministerial or hierarchical priesthood differ in essence and not just in degree, they are nonetheless ordered to one another" (*Lumen gentium*, no. 10; CCC 1547). But what does this difference in essence mean? Are priests essentially different from other baptized people? Did the Council not want to avoid giving too strong an emphasis to priests over and against the laity?

The simplest way of explaining what the Council is teaching here is to make a distinction between end and means. Everything in the Church is at the service of an end: to unite men in living communion with God and with one another. In other words, the whole goal of the Church is holiness: "This is the will of God, your sanctification" (1 Thess 4:3). Everything in the Church should serve this goal. The Church is, of course, not an end in herself, but, as the Council says, a "sacrament", that is, a "sign and instrument of innermost union with God and of unity among all men" (*Lumen gentium*, no. 1). We exercise our "common priesthood" through the unfolding of baptismal grace in our lives, in "a life of faith, hope, and charity, a life according to the Spirit" (CCC 1547). And so we can say this: The "common priesthood" becomes a living reality in the holiness of Christians.

The Church has means by which this life of grace can unfold—means that Christ instituted and the Church herself developed. The Word of God and the sacraments are such God-given "means of salvation". But the Church's institutions, canon law, and pastoral organizations are also means. They are all meant to serve the same end: the salvation of men, their sanctification and sanctity. Thus the ministerial priesthood is at the service of the common priesthood. "It is directed at the unfolding of the baptismal grace of all Christians. The ministerial priesthood is a *means* by which Christ unceasingly builds up and leads his Church. For this reason it is transmitted by its own sacrament, the sacrament of Holy Orders" (CCC 1547).

Now can we see why the priesthood is a ministry. "It is entirely related to Christ and to men", for the service of Christ in men. The "power" that ordination bestows is "none other than that of Christ" (CCC 1551). That is why Christ asked Peter three times whether he loved him before he three times commissioned him to tend his flock (Jn 21:15–17).

47

The ministry of deacons

The Second Vatican Council restored the diaconate in the Latin Church "as a proper and permanent rank of the hierarchy" (CCC 1571). Since then—more exactly, since 1970—in our diocese and in many other particular Churches throughout the world, there have been ordinations of "permanent deacons", who are often married men. A new reality has emerged in the life of the Church, and if we look back now on scarcely thirty years' experience, it is hard to imagine life without it.

But who is the deacon? What is the significance of his ministry? What is he ordained for? Many people think that this ministry is not really necessary, that lay people with special permission can do practically everything the deacon does. I think this is a rather superficial point of view. We should define the meaning of ordination not in terms of doing, of function, but first of all in terms of *being*.

The sacrament of holy orders always signifies a special kind of "configuration to Christ" (CCC 1581, 1585). The ordained man becomes the "living instrument" of Christ. "[I]t is ultimately Christ who acts and effects salvation through the ordained minister" (CCC 1584). The sacrament of holy orders places a man permanently in the service of Christ. The "officeholder" is more than a functionary. Ordination enables him, in his person and ministry, to represent Christ and to make him present. That is why we need the sacrament of holy orders—so that Christ as Shepherd and Head of his Church may be present and active through the ministry of those he has sent.

But how does the ordination of the deacon differ from the other degrees of ordination, of the bishop and the priest? Hands are laid on the deacon, says the Council, "not unto the priesthood, but unto the ministry" (CCC 1569). He is not ordained to the priesthood, but to the "ministry". The deacon is not an "incomplete priest", a preliminary stage on the way to the priesthood (even though all those who receive priestly ordination are first ordained as deacons). The deacon represents Christ, not as High Priest (which is why he does not offer the Sacrifice of the Mass), but as the One who came "not to be served but to serve" (Mk 10:45).

The priest and the deacon, each in his own way, are united through their ordination with the bishop: the former in the *presbyterium*, in the communion of priests as co-workers of the bishop (CCC 1562), and the latter as the bishop's helper in the many different kinds of *diakonia*, ministry to the poor, of the Word, at the altar. In parishes they are placed beside and under the priests as co-workers of the bishop.

The question is often posed today about the diaconate for women. In the early Church there were deaconesses. What was the significance of their ordination? What exactly was their ministry? Essentially nothing different from the one we see exercised today by women religious, extraordinary ministers of Communion, readers, and pastoral assistants. The crucial thing is always the same: to be willing to serve as Christ served.

48

The sacrament of matrimony

Marriage is, so to speak, "the most natural thing in the world", and, at the same time, between Christians, it is a sacrament. "The intimate community of life and love", which is what marriage means, is as old as mankind. It is not human culture's discovery but its presupposition. Of course, in many respects, it has changed over the course of the centuries, and yet essentially it has remained the same. Its deepest foundation is mentioned by the Council: "God himself is the author of marriage" (CCC 1603). Marriage is part of the order of creation. It is willed by God. That is what the very first chapter of the Bible tells us: God created man in his image, man and woman he created them (Gen 1:27). God blessed their union and made it fruitful (Gen 1:28).

This same passage conveys a crucial message about marriage: "God saw that it was good." Marriage is not a makeshift arrangement, a concession to human weakness, but the very "image and likeness of God". "Since God created him man and woman, their mutual love becomes an image of the absolute and unfailing love with which God loves man" (CCC 1604). But that also means that marriage and the family, in their essential form, must not be subjected to the whims of the state, at the free disposal of society. They are the foundation and presupposition of every flourishing community. "Authority, stability, and a life of relationships within the family constitute the foundations for freedom, security, and fraternity within society" (CCC 2207).

Marriage is under threat—and the threats of today are not the first it has faced. Ever since man and woman began to live together in the communion of marriage, there have been conflicts, dramas, infidelity, jealousy, domination, and the breakdown of relationships. The doctrine of the faith teaches us that these things are not due to marriage itself, are not "proof" that marriage is bad, but rather that married people, too, are sinners, burdened with original sin and its consequences, the first of which was the rupture of the original communion of man and woman in Paradise. The order of creation in marriage is disturbed but not destroyed (CCC 1608). God's will for marriage, for the communion of life of man and woman, and for its fruitfulness has not been frustrated, but it does need, arduously and painfully, to be rediscovered.

The whole of the Old Testament is a kind of school for man and woman, to enable them to learn anew God's original plan. In this way, the laws that protect and surround marriage become so many signposts to the happiness that was originally planned (CCC 1609). The Song of Songs sings of the beauty of love: this, it says, is how strongly and passionately God loves mankind (CCC 1611). The Bible can find no stronger image for the covenant between God and his people than nuptial, marital love. But only Christ reveals how high is the price of love: on the Cross he gave himself up for the Church, his Bride. From this source flow all the sacraments, including matrimony.

49

Yes forever?

"Love is strong as death, jealousy is cruel as the grave. Its flashes are flashes of fire, a most vehement flame. Many waters cannot quench love, neither can floods drown it. If a man offered for love all the wealth of his house, it would be utterly scorned." Those are the words of the Song of Songs (8:6–7) in the Old Testament (CCC 1611). Love is meant to last. That is an essential part of its dynamism. Love is meant to be faithful, permanent, complete—that is not something forced on love from outside. All the more painful, then, is the loss of love, the wounding of love.

According to Sacred Scripture, this profound "inclination to permanence" reflects the Creator's will for mankind. "Therefore a man leaves his father and his mother and cleaves to his wife, and they become one flesh" (Gen 2:24). "The Lord himself shows that this signifies an unbreakable union of their two lives by recalling what the plan of the Creator had been 'in the beginning': 'So they are no longer two, but one flesh' (Mt 19:6)" (CCC 1605).

"What therefore God has joined together, let not man put asunder" (Mt 19:6). These words of our Lord remind us that love is indeed meant to be permanent, but it is not permanent of itself. Love is endangered from within and from without. It can fade away, become a cold indifference, even turn into hatred. Nowadays, when this happens, we are inclined simply to "write the death certificate" of love. It just "died prematurely". But what we fail to see is that marriage has created a new reality, which continues to exist and survives even the dying off of emotions. Through the mutual Yes of matrimonial consent (CCC 1625), the "bond of marriage" has come into existence and unites the two spouses permanently. "[*T*]*he marriage bond* has been established by God himself in such a way that a marriage concluded and consummated between baptized persons can never be dissolved. This bond, which results from the free human act of the spouses and their consummation of the marriage, is a reality, henceforth irrevocable, and gives rise to a covenant guaranteed by God's fidelity" (CCC 1640). Neither society nor the Church nor the couple concerned has the power to dissolve this bond (CCC 1644).

In the realities of life this "Yes forever" often appears to be an excessive demand, an unlivable commandment. It is not for nothing that the disciples of Jesus are shocked by his words (cf. Mt 19:10). More and more frequently today relationships break down, even those regarded as exemplary. Single persons are increasing in number (CCC 1658), as are single parents. It is as if we were finding it harder to put up with one another. But how are we supposed to learn trust in human loyalty, if not first of all through being able to trust the "I will" of marriage once it has been given? "Spouses who with God's grace give this witness, often in very difficult conditions, deserve the gratitude and support of the ecclesial community" (CCC 1648). They provide great support and encouragement.

50

Yes to life

"When a woman is in travail she has sorrow, because her hour has come; but when she is delivered of the child, she no longer remembers the anguish, for joy that a child is born into the world" (Jn 16:21). In his Farewell Discourse, our Lord uses this fundamental human experience to give the disciples a vivid image for understanding the "hour" in which he and they find themselves shortly before his Passion. Sorrow and joy, grief and happiness are very close to one another. Cross and resurrection are like the pain and the joy of childbirth.

The "natural" human wonder of birth corresponds to the wonder of "rebirth" (Tit 3:5) through grace. "Joy that a child is born into the world" fills us, over and over again, with astonishment. It is one of the most natural things there is. No human being comes into the world except through conception and birth. Everyone is the child of his parents, however imperfect they may be, and no one sees the light of the world without a mother carrying this child of hers and giving him birth.

And yet in this very natural process, countless times repeated, something amazing happens time and again: an unmistakable and utterly unique being, a human person, created and willed and eternally loved by God, comes into existence. The immortal spiritual soul, which makes man a person, is created immediately by God at the very moment when life begins (CCC 366).

The exceedingly serious responsibility of transmitting human life makes spouses "free and conscious collaborators of God the Creator" (*Humanae vitae*). There is no natural human act through which human beings so directly, mysteriously, and authentically cooperate in the creative work of God than the act of transmitting life. As Pope John Paul II says: "At the beginning of every human person there stands a creative act on the part of God. No human being comes into life by chance; he is always the purpose of God's creative love." Only this great and yet entirely realistic view of man enables us to see what is involved in the transmission of human life: "From this fundamental truth of faith and reason it follows that the generative power inscribed into human sexuality . . . is a cooperation with the creative power of God" (Address, *L'Osservatore romano*, September 18, 1983).

However controversial *Humanae vitae* may be, however much it was and is disputed, the encyclical's essential point—the irrevocable inner connection of the union of love and the transmission of life—can be understood at the deepest level only in this perspective: conjugal love is always ordered to fecundity, even when through responsible parenthood (CCC 2368) or for physical reasons (CCC 1654) it does not or cannot lead to the transmission of life. The Dominican Father Molinié writes: "We are one, because love makes one; we are two, because love shows respect; we are three, because love goes beyond itself."

51

A many-colored garland: the sacramentals

What would the sacraments be, these great signs of salvation, without the many little "sacred signs", actions and things, that surround the sacraments like a many-colored garland? Whenever anyone goes into church, he takes holy water and makes on himself the sign of the Cross. Is it being trivial to feel the lack of these signs as a deficiency? Is it "ignorance" if certain sacred signs—for example, the Advent wreath or the blessing of herbs—enjoy a growing popularity? Where there is a dearth of sacred signs, other things, often superstitious, take their place, such as mascots in cars or knocking on wood.

They have been called "sacramentals" ever since the Church clearly designated the seven "great" sacred signs that are the sacraments. They enjoy a certain proximity to the sacraments; they are, as it were, the "outskirts" of the sacraments. If we approach them only with the question of whether they are absolutely "necessary", whether we can manage without them, then we miss their whole point. This is what the Council says about them: "Holy Mother Church has, moreover, instituted sacramentals. These are sacred signs which bear a resemblance to the sacraments. They signify effects, particularly of a spiritual nature, which are obtained through the intercession of the Church. By them men are disposed to receive the chief effect of the sacraments, and various occasions in life are rendered holy" (CCC 1667).

Sacramentals are not magic tricks. They always have the character of prayer and therefore of petition to God for particular helps and graces, for his blessing. They are signs of God's blessing in the very varied circumstances of life (CCC 1668). Blessing is a task and service for all the baptized. All of us are supposed to "be a blessing" (Gen 12:2). Making the sign of the Cross on the brow of a child or of someone we love, crossing ourselves, grace before and after meals, sprinkling with holy water are all such gestures of blessing.

The language of the Church distinguishes, though not too rigidly, between blessings and consecrations. Things and persons dedicated totally to God by way of sign are said to be consecrated. Things and persons are blessed when, at the Church's intercession, they are placed under God's special protection (CCC 1671–72). "Here are some examples. Churches and cemeteries are consecrated places; altars and bells are consecrated things; abbots and abbesses are consecrated persons. Blessed places include houses and fields of crops. Blessed persons include the sick, the elderly, married couples. Blessed things include cars, herbs, fruit, and so on" (H. Vorgrimler, *Sakramententheologie* [Düsseldorf 1992], 345). "Only things that can be put to a good use and are not ambiguous may be blessed" (ibid., 346). All the more important is the sacred duty of all Christians, wherever they may be, to bring blessing, to counteract the un-blessing of evil, to bring peace and healing, and to be a reminder that everything rests on the blessing of God.

52

Wellsprings flowing into eternal life

We have reached the end of our journey through the world of the sacraments. For a whole year, week by week, we have followed the great contours of the *Catechism* and meditated on the sevenfold wellspring that is the sacraments. In this final meditation we shall look once more at the "sacramental economy" (CCC 1076) as a whole.

The key to a deep understanding of the world of the sacraments is the mystery of the Incarnation of God, the God-manhood of Jesus Christ. Just as in Christ his humanity, his concrete human existence, was and is the "instrument of salvation", the living instrument of his divinity, so the sacraments are in a certain way the instruments of Christ, through which He, by means of human signs, bestows his own life upon us.

The sacraments have their primal source "above, where Christ is, seated at the right hand of God" (Col 3:1). They stream forth from eternal life into this world and time, and if we accept them and let them have their effect in us, then "rivers of living water" will flow from within us (Jn 7:38), and these rivers will overflow into eternal life.

The sacraments—to use an image of the Greek mystic and layman, Saint Nicolaus Cabasilas—are the "gates of righteousness" (Ps 117:19) through which the "King of glory", Jesus Christ, continues to make his entrance into this world. Through his death and Resurrection Christ has opened these gates and now comes unfailingly through them to us. And only through these gates can we reach him (Nicolaus Cabasilas, *The Life in Christ* [Crestwood, N.Y.: St. Vladimir's Seminary Press, 1974]).

As long as we are pilgrims on earth, as long as "we are at home in the body . . . [and] away from the Lord" (2 Cor 5:6), the sacraments, the sacred signs of Christ, are for us the gates to life, the wellsprings from which the life of Christ flows out to us. Because these sacramental signs are so modest, so unobtrusive and inconspicuous, it requires humility to discover in them the wellsprings that flow from above. Christ is not tied to his sacraments. He can give his grace without coming through the gates of the sacraments. That is why the Church believes that Christ can bestow what baptism effects—regeneration to new life—even without the outward sign of baptism. But we rely for entry on these gates. We have to bend our pride and enter through these humble, lowly gates (CCC 1257).

Only when we have gone through the last gate, through death, do the signs cease, the signs that have accompanied and strengthened us throughout our earthly life, from baptism to the last anointing with the oil of the sick (CCC 1523). Let us hope and pray that at that time we may enter into the light that knows no setting, where Christ no longer meets us veiled beneath sacramental signs, and that we may gaze upon him in glory without veil. But even now, thanks to the sacraments, we are "united with Christ" and thus with all those who are already perfectly in his presence (CCC 1690).